50 things you can do today to boost your self-esteem

Foreword by Professor Cary L. Cooper, CBE,
Distinguished Professor of Organizational Psychology
and Health at Lancaster University

Wendy Green

PERSONAL HEALTH GUIDES

summersdale

50 THINGS YOU CAN DO TODAY TO BOOST YOUR SELF-ESTEEM

Summersdale Publishers Ltd
46 West Street
Chichester
West Sussex
PO19 1RP
UK

www.summersdale.com

Printed and bound by CPI Group (UK) Ltd, Croydon, CR0 4YY

ISBN: 978-1-84953-405-5

Substantial discounts on bulk quantities of Summersdale books are available to corporations, professional associations and other organisations. For details contact Nicky Douglas by telephone: +44 (0) 1243 756902, fax: +44 (0) 1243 786300 or email: nicky@summersdale.com.

Disclaimer
Every effort has been made to ensure that the information in this book is accurate and current at the time of publication. The author and the publisher cannot accept responsibility for any misuse or misunderstanding of any information contained herein, or any loss, damage or injury, be it health, financial or otherwise, suffered by any individual or group acting upon or relying on information contained herein. None of the opinions or suggestions in this book is intended to replace medical opinion. If you have concerns about your health, please seek professional advice.

To my husband Gordon, thanks for
being so supportive, and to my grandsons
– Scott, Dylan and Kieran

Acknowledgements

I would like to thank Claire Plimmer for commissioning this title. I'd also like to thank Professor Cary L. Cooper, Distinguished Professor of Organizational Psychology and Health at Lancaster University, for kindly agreeing to write the foreword. Thanks also to Anna Martin and Elanor Clarke for their very helpful editorial input.

Other titles in the Personal Health Guides series include:

50 Things You Can Do Today to Boost Your Confidence
50 Things You Can Do Today to Increase Your Fertility
50 Things You Can Do Today to Manage Anxiety
50 Things You Can Do Today to Manage Arthritis
50 Things You Can Do Today to Manage Back Pain
50 Things You Can Do Today to Manage Eczema
50 Things You Can Do Today to Manage Fibromyalgia
50 Things You Can Do Today to Manage Hay Fever
50 Things You Can Do Today to Manage IBS
50 Things You Can Do Today to Manage Insomnia
50 Things You Can Do Today to Manage Menopause
50 Things You Can Do Today to Manage Migraines
50 Things You Can Do Today to Manage Stress

Contents

Chapter 7 – Aspire and Achieve **115**

**Chapter 8 – Get the Feel-Good Factor with
DIY Complementary Therapies** **128**

Author's Note

Twenty years ago I was a divorced mother of two, living on benefits in a council house and I didn't envisage ever having much of a career. It was only when I met someone who decided to go to university as a mature student that I began to realise there were opportunities out there for me too. Gradually I turned my life around by going to university and studying for a BSc Honours degree in health studies.

When I started my degree I was convinced that it was too difficult for me, that everyone else on the course was cleverer than me and that I would never manage to complete it. However, I surprised myself in the first year when I passed my coursework and exams with flying colours. My success gave me the confidence to carry on, even though I still felt that I would never manage to attain a degree.

What I found was that every time I achieved a good mark my self-esteem and self-belief grew. When I achieved a first class honours degree I finally began to see myself as a reasonably intelligent and capable person; this gave me the confidence to enrol on a teaching in further education course, which I felt would give me the best chance of finding a decent job. I found the teaching practice in higher and further education terrifying, but I was determined to complete the course. Once I passed, I applied for a tutor's post in my local college and got it. Since then I have held posts in the voluntary sector in mentoring and health promotion and am the author of fourteen books. I now believe that anyone can do anything they set their mind to; I think the key to high self-esteem is to look after your mind and body and to acknowledge, use and develop your strengths and talents.

Wendy Green

Foreword

by Professor Cary L. Cooper, CBE, Distinguished Professor
of Organizational Psychology and Health at
Lancaster University

A recent report by the Centre for the Modern Family showed that 76 per cent of families are worried about their current financial situation and, given the dire consequences of the continuing economic downturn throughout the world, i.e. job losses, lack of job security and financial instability, the issue of a person's self-esteem has become a top priority. These scenarios can lead to the undermining of an individual's sense of security and wellbeing, and ultimately their self-esteem.

This book provides practical solutions to enhance people's self-esteem, suggestions that are within everybody's control. Feeling physically and emotionally fit to confront life's challenges is essential not just to survive, but to flourish. Taking control of your life and embracing change are fundamental steps to ensuring increased self-esteem and greater self-confidence. This book will provide you with the ammunition to begin this process... listen and engage with its sound advice.

Introduction

This book explains what self-esteem is, as well as what affects it, and offers practical advice and a holistic approach to help you boost yours.

Low self-esteem can have a negative impact on your aspirations, achievements and relationships, and cause self-destructive behaviours, such as eating disorders or drug and alcohol addictions. If you suffer from low self-esteem it is vital that you take steps to improve it if you want to lead a happy, healthy life and reach your full potential.

Taking care of your physical and mental health is both a sign of strong self-esteem and a self-esteem builder. Within this book we will examine how a wholesome diet, regular exercise and effective stress management can improve your self-esteem, which in turn will benefit every aspect of your life.

Learn how to boost your self-esteem by accepting and valuing yourself, as well as taking pride in your strengths, talents and achievements. You'll also discover how positive self-talk (the continuous conversation you have with yourself) can change your self-image, and how to increase your self-esteem by setting and achieving goals.

There's also a selection of relaxation techniques and complementary therapy treatments, which you can try for yourself for that feel-good factor. At the end of the book you'll find recipes based on the dietary guidelines set out in the book, as well as details of helpful products, books and organisations.

Chapter 1

About Self-Esteem

In this chapter we will define what self-esteem is, how it is developed and what the effects of low and high self-esteem are.

1. Learn about self-esteem

What is self-esteem?

Self-esteem is basically how highly you rate yourself in terms of worthiness, appearance and competence. If you have mainly negative beliefs about yourself and your abilities, your self-esteem will be low. On the other hand, if you generally view yourself as a worthy, attractive and capable person your self-esteem will be high. Your self-esteem forms the blueprint of how you think, feel and act, so it has far-reaching effects on every aspect of your life – from your personal relationships and social life to your career and health.

How does self-esteem develop?

Your self-esteem is the result of the beliefs you have formed about yourself in response to your experiences and relationships at home, at school, at work and in your personal life.

During childhood, when you were developing your individual personality and sense of self, you were especially vulnerable to the effects of negative experiences, which can leave you with the belief that you are unimportant or worthless. The kinds of childhood experiences that can have an impact on your self-esteem include:

- Emotional or physical neglect (e.g. lack of affection, not enough food, etc.)

- Feeling that you have failed to meet your parents' or teachers' expectations

- Negative feedback from a parent or teacher

- Difficulty in forming friendships with other pupils at school

- Being bullied

- Emotional, physical, or sexual abuse

What keeps low self-esteem going?

When you have negative beliefs about yourself your self-talk is also likely to be negative. Self-talk is the constant internal dialogue you have with yourself and it has a direct effect on your self-worth. Positive self-talk, such as 'I am a likeable person' or 'I can do whatever I put my mind to', generates high self-esteem; whereas negative self-talk, such as 'I don't deserve to be loved' or 'I'm hopeless', is likely to result in low self-esteem.

What are the effects of low self-esteem?

Low self-esteem can manifest itself in various ways including:

Problematic relationships
If you suffer from poor self-esteem you may form damaging relationships – especially if you suffered from emotional, physical or sexual abuse as a child. You may allow your partner and friends to treat you badly because you don't believe you deserve to be treated with love and respect. Also, research suggests that if you have been the victim of abuse you are more likely to become an abuser yourself and engage in aggressive or violent behaviour.

Diminished social life
If you have a low opinion about yourself – especially of your appearance and your ability to interact with others – you may avoid going to social events because you're too shy or embarrassed, or because you're overly sensitive to other people's comments and opinions about you.

Low aspirations
If you have low self-esteem you will lack the self-belief to aim high at school, in your career, and in terms of your lifestyle, health and relationships. As a result, you might set your sights low in each of these areas and fail to reach your full potential.

Underachievement
Low self-esteem is likely to lead to underachievement at school and in your career. If you don't believe you can achieve things in life, you are unlikely to even try.

Failure to reach your full potential at work
If your low self-esteem stems from the belief that you are incompetent or unintelligent, you might not apply for the jobs you'd like to do, or attend interviews, because you don't think you're good enough.

If you have a job you might worry about your performance and not stand up for yourself, which could stop you from climbing the career ladder and make you vulnerable to workplace bullying.

Self-destructive behaviours
You might attempt to cope with your low self-esteem by trying to 'escape' from life by eating too much or too little, drinking too much or taking drugs, which could lead to related health problems. You might become aggressive or even violent to hide your own vulnerabilities and to protect yourself from further damage.

Negative outlook
When your self-esteem is low you are likely to have a negative outlook – it's hard to feel positive about your life and future when you feel negative about yourself.

Anxiety
When your self-belief is low you're more likely to worry about things like your appearance or what other people think of you.

What affects self-esteem?

Self-esteem is not static – it can fluctuate in line with your current beliefs about yourself. Your self-belief can change throughout your life according to your current circumstances and experiences. The mass media also play a part with their constant portrayal of how we should look, feel and act, and the material goods we should own in order to be considered successful in today's society. If you don't feel that you measure up to these ideals it's easy to fall into the trap of feeling as though you're not quite good enough.

Significant negative life events in adult life and how you deal with them can also change your core beliefs about yourself. This may happen over a period of time and you might not even realise that your self-esteem has taken a knock. Experiences that often have a negative impact on people's self-esteem include:

- Workplace bullying or excessive work pressures

- Emotional or physical trauma – for example, divorce/end of a relationship or injury

- Physical ill-health

- Dissatisfaction with the way you look

- Being overweight/underweight

- Low mood and depression

- Bereavement

- Redundancy/unemployment

- Loneliness/social isolation

- Excessive pressure (i.e. stress)

What are the effects of high self-esteem?

No one can feel happy all of the time and having high self-esteem doesn't mean you will always be successful in your career and relationships, but if you have high self-esteem you are more likely to feel happy, fulfilled and content with your life. People with high self-esteem tend to trust their own judgement and ability to solve problems. They accept and like themselves as they are and don't feel the need to compare themselves with other people in terms of their abilities, appearance and financial status. They feel valued and respected by other people. They enjoy the challenge of setting and achieving goals and can handle negative feedback. They generally feel positive and upbeat about life, are more able to remain optimistic and bounce back when things go wrong and are therefore less likely to suffer from stress.

How can I boost my self-esteem?

The good news is, as already mentioned, your self-esteem isn't fixed – just as it can fall from time to time due to negative events and experiences, it can also rise.

You can build your self-esteem by taking good care of your physical and mental health with a healthy diet, exercise, and taking steps to manage stress and sleep well. Taking good care of yourself will result in glowing skin, gleaming hair and a trim body, which will help you to feel more confident about your appearance. Learning how to accept and value yourself for who you are, and becoming more assertive to encourage others to treat you with the respect you deserve, will also raise your self-esteem.

The beliefs you hold about yourself underpin your self-esteem – but beliefs are just opinions, not facts, and they can be changed.

Focusing on your strengths, positive qualities and achievements, so that you see yourself as a worthy, capable and competent person, will improve your self-belief. Using positive self-talk and affirmations will also increase your self-belief, raise your aspirations and help you to achieve your goals, which will in turn help your self-esteem to grow. Using techniques from complementary therapies such as aromatherapy and the emotional freedom techniques (EFT) could also help you to feel better about yourself. This book offers you practical advice in each of these areas to help you develop strong, resilient self-esteem.

Self-esteem assessment tool

As well as fluctuating according to your current circumstances, your self-esteem can vary from one area of your life to another. For example, one person might believe they are a very good parent, yet lack confidence in a work environment; whereas another might view themselves as competent in their job, but feel awkward in social situations.

Complete the self-assessment chart on page 19 to ascertain your self-esteem in various roles. You'll probably find that your self-esteem fluctuates quite a bit depending on the situation, for example: you might rate yourself eight out of ten as a parent but only five out of ten as an employee. Complete the chart again in a few weeks' time, after you have practised some of the self-esteem-building techniques in this book, to help you gauge whether you have improved your self-esteem.

Rate yourself out of ten:

Your self-esteem rating…	Date	Rating out of ten	Date	Rating out of ten
As a friend				
As a parent				
As a grandparent				
As a spouse/partner				
As a sibling				
As an employee/ pupil/ manager/ teacher				
On your appearance				

Chapter 2

Feed Your Self-Esteem

Most of us realise there is a link between what we eat and our physical health, but few of us consider the effect our diet can have on our emotional wellbeing. Research by Mind and the Mental Health Foundation suggests that our eating habits affect how the brain works and its structure, which in turn influence mood and behaviour.

The Mental Health Foundation's *Feeding Minds* report in 2006 linked the increasing incidence of mental health problems, such as low mood and depression, in the UK to changes in our diets; it's thought that we eat only two-thirds of the fruit and vegetables and less than half the amount of fish we did 60 years ago. Other studies back this up, claiming that eating a diet rich in fruit, vegetables, fish, nuts and whole grain cereals helps to prevent depression and promote physical health. Since self-esteem is closely linked to mood and emotional wellbeing, as well as physical health, it seems sensible to assume that eating this type of diet will provide the foundations on which to build positive self-esteem.

Good nutrition will also help you to make the most of your appearance; if you eat a balanced diet you are more likely to maintain a healthy weight, have glowing skin and glossy hair; if you are happy with your weight and general appearance you are more likely to have a positive self-image.

We will also look at supplements that may help to boost mood and therefore improve self-esteem. Supplements are controversial, with some researchers arguing that isolated substances don't provide the same benefits the nutrients found naturally in foods do; this is partly because foods provide a range of nutrients that interact with each other. However, if you struggle to eat a balanced diet – for whatever reason – supplements can help to protect you from nutritional deficiencies and provide you with the health benefits of particular herbs, vitamins and minerals.

2. Balance your mood with complex carbs

For healthy self-esteem you need to balance your mood in order to avoid emotional 'ups and downs'. To achieve this you need to keep your blood-sugar levels steady by eating foods that break down into glucose (sugar) slowly; the brain uses up more glucose than any other organ and needs a continuous supply to keep it running smoothly. Complex (unrefined) carbohydrates, such as whole grains, fruit, vegetables and pulses produce slow and steady rises in blood glucose.

It's best to avoid processed foods and drinks in your diet, such as white bread, pastries, sugary drinks and sweets, as these are easily turned into glucose, causing your blood sugar to rapidly peak and then trough. Low blood sugar not only triggers mood swings, but also leads to poor concentration, fatigue and irritability.

Good examples of complex carbohydrates include multigrain bread, porridge, whole wheat pasta, brown basmati rice, apples, cherries, plums, bananas (the less ripe the better), sweet potatoes, carrots, beans, peas and lentils.

The fibre in these foods slows down the rate at which they are digested. These foods also supply the vitamins and minerals you need for a happy disposition. Not only that, but because these foods take longer to digest, more energy is expended during the process, which helps to cut calories and prevent weight gain.

How foods are cooked is also important. New potatoes boiled in their skins are broken down more slowly than mashed potato. Pasta that is cooked *al dente* takes longer to digest than pasta that is cooked until it is soft.

Eating regularly also helps to maintain your blood-sugar levels. If you're hungry in between meals try snacking on oatcakes with cottage cheese, a handful of nuts or seeds, an apple or an orange. Keeping your blood sugar stable also helps you to control your weight. As mentioned above, maintaining a healthy weight is important not just for your physical health but also your self-esteem; being overweight can have a hugely negative impact on self-esteem.

3. Enjoy 'happy hormone' boosting proteins

Eating protein-rich foods like eggs, fish, poultry, low-fat dairy foods, lean meats, nuts, seeds, beans and lentils, alongside unrefined carbohydrates, helps to boost your mood and therefore your self-esteem in three key ways:

1. Proteins slow down the rate at which glucose is released into the bloodstream, helping to balance mood.

2. Proteins supply the amino acids tryptophan and phenylalanine, which the brain uses to make the self-esteem enhancing 'happy hormone' serotonin, and the 'motivating hormones' dopamine, noradrenalin and adrenalin.

3. Complex carbohydrates help the brain to absorb the tryptophan and phenylalanine in protein foods.

4. Eat the right fats

Your brain is roughly 60 per cent fat, so you need to eat enough fat for it to work efficiently; studies suggest that low-fat diets can cause depression and therefore could be implicated in low self-esteem. However, you need to make sure you eat the right types and amounts of fat.

Types of fats

The foods we eat supply four types of fat – saturated, polyunsaturated (omega-3 and omega-6), trans and monounsaturated (omega-9).

Saturated fats – mainly found in animal products like red meat, butter and full-fat dairy products such as cream, cheese and milk. They are solid at room temperature and are thought to raise harmful LDL (low-density lipoprotein) cholesterol levels; these are believed to make the brain cells less flexible and lead to atherosclerosis (hardening of the arteries), raising the risk of heart disease and strokes. They may also make it more difficult for the brain to use polyunsaturated fats. You should aim to cut back on foods that are high in saturated fats by choosing low-fat versions of dairy foods and leaner cuts of meat. Eat processed foods such as pies, cakes, biscuits and ready meals sparingly, and go for lower-fat versions – check the label: 3 per cent and under = low fat; 20 per cent and over = high fat.

Polyunsaturated fats – called essential fatty acids (EFAs) because, unlike other fatty acids, the body can't produce them – so we need to get them from food. They are largely obtained from fish, vegetable oils, nuts and seeds. There are two main kinds of EFAs: omega-3, found in oily fish, nuts, seeds and certain plant seed oils, such as flax seed oil and rapeseed oil; omega-6, found in plant seed oils like sunflower, sesame and pumpkin oils, corn oil, nuts, seeds and meat. Both omega-3 and omega-6 fatty acids are vital for proper brain function.

Long-chain and short-chain fatty acids – there are two types of omega-3 fatty acids – long-chain and short-chain. Long-chain fatty acids include eicosapentaenoic acid (EPA) and docosahexaenoic acid (DHA), which are obtained from oily fish like sardines, pilchards, mackerel, herring, salmon and fresh (not tinned) tuna. Researchers blame the UK's lower intake of fish in recent years for an increase in mood disorders such as depression, seasonal affective disorder (SAD), post-natal depression and bipolar disorder, all of which are associated with low self-esteem.

Short-chain fatty acids include alpha-linoleic acid (ALA); rich sources are flaxseed oil, rapeseed oil, pumpkin seeds, walnuts, whole grains, wheat germ and soya beans. The body can also get EPA and DHA from these – but in smaller amounts.

Get the balance right

Aim to get the right balance between the two essential fatty acids – too much omega-6 can hamper the body's ability to break down omega-3 oils and has been linked with depression. UK diets tend to supply too much omega-6 because many processed foods, cooking oils and margarines contain corn oil and sunflower oil. To counteract this, eat more oily fish and replace sunflower oil, corn cooking oils and margarines with olive oil, or rapeseed oil and margarines based on these oils. Use flax seed oil as a salad dressing, and snack on walnuts and pumpkin seeds.

Trans fats – also known as partially hydrogenated fats, are solid fats, which are manufactured from liquid vegetable oils using a process called hydrogenation. It's thought that if you eat a lot of these fats they replace polyunsaturated fats in the brain with harmful effects. Trans fats have also been linked to weight gain – especially around the tummy, which is a risk factor for heart disease and diabetes. Trans fats tend to be used in some margarines and processed foods like biscuits, pies and cakes to help extend their shelf life, so the best way to lower your intake is to eat these foods sparingly, or opt for products that state they don't contain hydrogenated fats on the packaging.

Monounsaturated fats – also known as omega-9 fats, are mainly found in olive, rapeseed and groundnut oils, avocados, nuts and seeds. They play a vital part in brain function because they are involved in the production and release of the learning and memory neurotransmitter acetylcholine, and they also lower LDL cholesterol.

5. Have an ACE diet

Eating plenty of fresh fruit and vegetables will ensure your diet is rich in antioxidants, such as beta carotene (a type of vitamin A), and vitamins C and E. Antioxidants are thought to counteract the damaging effects of pollutants (oxidants) on cells in the brain and the rest of the body – protecting memory and boosting immunity to disease. Vitamin A is also found as retinol in animal products such as liver, cod or halibut liver oils, egg yolks, whole milk, cheese and butter. Rich sources of vitamin C include blackcurrants, citrus fruits, berries, peppers (especially red), tomatoes, broccoli, kale, potatoes, peas and cabbage. Vitamin C is also obtained from lamb, beef and chicken livers. Vitamin E is present in berries (in the seeds), avocados and sweet potatoes, as well as in nuts, seeds, olive oil and whole grains.

Eating fruit and vegetables across the spectrum of colours provides you with a wide range of nutrients and antioxidants. For example, the antioxidant beta carotene gives apricots, carrots, sweet potatoes, butternut squash and peppers their orange/red shades; another type of antioxidant called anthocyanins give fruits such as blueberries, blackcurrants, plums, raspberries and strawberries their blue, purple and red hues. The deeper the colour the more anthocyanins the fruit contains. Green vegetables such as broccoli, kale and spinach are rich in the antioxidants beta-carotene and lutein. Lutein also gives sweetcorn its yellow colour.

Fruit and vegetables also supply other nutrients, such as B vitamins and various minerals that your body needs to make neurotransmitters (chemicals that transmit messages throughout the brain and nervous system). Thus eating at least five portions of fruit and vegetables daily helps to promote optimum mental and physical health, the cornerstones of strong self-esteem.

6. Lift your mood with B vitamins

All of the B vitamins are important for good mental health. Diets low in vitamins B1 (thiamine), B3 (niacin) and B5 (pantothenic acid) have been linked with low mood and depression. Vitamin B6 (pyridoxine) is needed by the body to produce both serotonin and GABA (gamma-aminobutyric acid); a shortage of either of these neurotransmitters can contribute to depression. Vitamin B9 (folic acid or folate) deficiency is associated with depressive symptoms. Both folic acid and vitamin B12 are needed by the body to produce SAMe (S-adenosyl-L-methionine) – a chemical the body uses to make neurotransmitters. A lack of biotin (also known as vitamin B7 vitamin H or coenzyme R) has been linked with depression and panic attacks.

A general lack of B vitamins in the diet is linked to high levels of homocysteine, an amino acid found naturally in the body. There is strong evidence that the higher your homocysteine levels are, the more likely you are to suffer from depression and physical illnesses such as heart disease, stroke and cancer.

A balanced diet of meat, fish, eggs, dairy foods, whole grains, vegetables – including green leafy vegetables (such as cabbage, broccoli, Brussels sprouts, lettuce, rocket and spinach), beetroot and mushrooms – as well as citrus fruits, beans, peas, lentils, nuts and seeds, should provide sufficient B vitamins for most people's requirements. Marmite is also an excellent source of B vitamins. If you're a vegan, or if you eat a lot of processed foods, you could be deficient. Also, if you're under stress, your body's need for these nutrients increases dramatically. In any of these situations taking a vitamin B complex supplement may be beneficial.

Grapefruit alert

Grapefruit is a good source of vitamins A and C, calcium and magnesium, but recent research shows it can interact with a number of commonly prescribed drugs, increasing their potency and the risk of dangerous side effects, or reducing their effectiveness. If you have been prescribed certain anti-cancer, anti-clotting, anti-psychotic or anti-nausea drugs, antibiotics, cholesterol or blood-pressure-lowering drugs, certain painkillers or anti-rejection immunosuppressants, your GP and/or pharmacist should have warned you of these dangers. If in doubt, check the accompanying patient information leaflet, or speak to your GP or pharmacist.

7. Put the D in your diet

A growing body of research suggests that vitamin D plays a vital role in both our physical and mental health. A lack of vitamin D may cause low mood because it's linked to low serotonin levels. A shortage can also leave you susceptible to infections because it lowers immunity. Suffering from repeated infections could have a negative effect on your mood and general health, and therefore affect your self-esteem.

Vitamin D also helps the body to absorb calcium, which is needed for a happy disposition (see page 30). In 2006 a three-month trial at the Queen Charlotte Hospital, London, suggested that eating a calcium and vitamin D-rich diet reduced PMS symptoms, including depression, irritability and fatigue, by about a third. Our main source of vitamin D is the sun – the skin makes a form of the vitamin after exposure to sunlight; thirty minutes of sunlight daily (without sun cream) should provide enough vitamin D for most people. However, with the UK climate this isn't always possible; a study in 2007 claimed that 60 per cent of middle-aged British adults had low levels of vitamin D and 16 per cent had a severe deficiency during the winter months.

The lack of sunshine in the UK means it's vital that you include more vitamin D in your diet. The best food sources by far are oily fish, with herrings providing the most, followed by pilchards, mackerel, salmon and sardines. Other reasonable sources include liver, butter, eggs, fortified margarines, cereals, powdered milk and orange juice, as well as mushrooms. The recommended daily intake is between 10 and 15 micrograms – one rollmop herring or two canned pilchards provide this amount. Supplementation is recommended if you don't eat vitamin D-rich foods regularly or if you can't get out in sunlight. If you decide to take a fish liver oil supplement don't take a multivitamin tablet as well, as vitamin D is fat-soluble, which means any excess is stored in the liver and fatty tissues; high levels can be harmful and may even cause depression.

Stay safe in the sun

If you are fair skinned and burn easily, expose your skin for ten minutes at a time, three times a day. Tip: Protect your skin from the damaging effects of the sun by eating dishes with tomato-based sauces. Research suggests that lycopene, an antioxidant in tomatoes that protects the plant from sunlight, does the same for us. Cooking tomatoes releases the lycopene from the cell walls, making it easier to absorb. Guavas, pink grapefruits and watermelons also contain lycopene.

Remember, overexposure to the sun's rays is linked to skin cancer, so make sure you apply a sun cream with a minimum sun protection factor (SPF) of 30 if you stay in the sun for longer than thirty minutes.

---

8. Mind your minerals

Minerals are nutrients that your brain and the rest of your body need in tiny amounts in order to function efficiently. Below is an overview of the key minerals your brain needs for a positive outlook on life:

Calming calcium

Calcium is needed for a calm disposition. If your diet is low in calcium you're likely to feel tense, irritable and find it hard to relax or sleep soundly – all of which could have an impact on your self-esteem.

Dairy foods are rich in calcium, especially low-fat milk and cheeses such as Edam, hard cheeses like Parmesan or Padano and yogurt. A 200 ml glass of any type of milk, plus a 150 g pot of low-fat plain yogurt and a 30 g piece of hard cheese would supply the 700 mg daily intake that is recommended in the UK for adults.

Calcium-fortified soya alternatives are also a good option. Other good sources include tinned sardines (if you eat the bones), almonds, seeds, dried apricots, oranges, oats, Brazil nuts, molasses, watercress, leeks, parsnips, lentils, beans – especially red kidney beans – green leafy vegetables, broccoli and celery. Calcium is also found in tap water – especially in hard-water areas – and in some bottled waters. Like vitamin D, the 'good' bacteria (lactobacillus, bifidobacterium and acidophilus) found in natural and bio yogurts, probiotic drinks,

Tip: Try a sprinkle of vinegar

Sprinkling leafy green vegetables with vinegar helps your body absorb the calcium they contain; the acetic acid in the vinegar helps break down foods and neutralises substances called oxalates, which block calcium absorption. Drinking a tablespoon of cider vinegar and honey in water once or twice daily is also thought to help calcium absorption, for the same reasons. Vinegar also helps to stabilise blood-sugar levels by slowing down glucose absorption.

tablets, capsules and powders that can be stirred into drinks or sprinkled over food, help the body absorb calcium. Interestingly, research has found a link between the level of good bacteria in the gut and mood. Scientists are unsure why this is the case, but one theory is that they boost the production of neurotransmitters. Prebiotics promote the growth of these beneficial bacteria in the gut and are found in garlic, leeks, onions, cucumber, celery and bananas.

Magnesium

Too little magnesium can lead to low mood. Magnesium is needed to use energy from foods and to transmit messages around the nervous system. It also helps the body to absorb calcium. If you're stressed or eat a lot of sugary foods, your magnesium levels could be low. To improve your magnesium intake, eat whole grains including wholemeal bread, brown rice and bran or whole wheat cereals, as well as oats, nuts and seeds, and dark-green leafy vegetables such as savoy cabbage, spinach, broccoli, chard or kale. Baked beans, peas, potatoes, fish, dairy foods and dark chocolate are also good everyday sources. You can also soak up magnesium through your skin by adding one or two cups of Epsom salts to the bath as it fills. Avoid drinking too much alcohol, as it can hamper magnesium absorption, (see Action 10). Fizzy drinks are also best avoided, because they contain phosphates, which also hinder magnesium absorption.

Chromium

Chromium helps to boost mood by keeping the blood sugar steady; it does this by working with insulin to take excess glucose from the blood. Good sources of chromium include chicken, beef, liver, eggs, whole grains like oats and wholemeal bread, apples, bananas, tomatoes, green peppers, broccoli, potatoes, spinach, onions and lentils. Reasonable sources include black pepper, dried basil and thyme.

Iron

Iron is involved in carrying oxygen around the body and a lack of it can contribute to low mood and fatigue. Women, vegetarians, vegans and dieters are especially at risk of having low iron levels. The best sources include, liver, shellfish – especially mussels and oysters – sardines, meat and poultry, dried fruit (especially apricots), dark-green leafy vegetables, such as chard and spinach, and the spice turmeric.

Selenium

Selenium affects how neurotransmitters work and is an antioxidant. Research published in *The Lancet* found a link between a lack of selenium and low mood.

Good sources of selenium include whole grains, eggs, fish, meat, poultry, Brazil nuts, cashew nuts, sunflower seeds, lentils, wheat germ, garlic, mushrooms and brewer's yeast.

Zinc

The brain and body use zinc to produce neurotransmitters. A shortage of zinc in the diet has been linked with low mood, anxiety and a lack of motivation and concentration – all of which could have a negative effect on self-esteem. Good sources of zinc include meat, fish and seafood, such as mussels and prawns, eggs, dairy foods, nuts, seeds, beans, mushrooms, broccoli, squash, spinach, kiwi fruit and blackberries.

Kitchen cupboard boosters

Enhance your self-esteem with these mood and brain-power-boosting herbs, spices and fruits from your kitchen cupboard.

 Basil booster – This pungent Mediterranean herb is used by herbalists to boost mood and relieve stress. Throw torn basil leaves over pizzas, salads and pasta. Add finely chopped leaves to summer fruit pudding.

Cinnamon soother – Cinnamon keeps blood-sugar levels steady for stable mood and energy levels and stimulates the brain. Sprinkle it over a cappuccino or latte, a bowl of porridge or baked apples.

Lemon aid – Sip freshly squeezed lemon juice in hot water to soothe away stress. Lemons contain linalool which, according to research at the University of Shizuoka, Japan, in 2007, dramatically cuts the body's stress response when it's inhaled.

Pep up with peppermint – Peppermint promotes clear thinking and alertness. Try drinking peppermint tea, or add finely chopped mint to salads and dressings, as well as to cold drinks in the summer.

Rosemary relaxer – This aromatic herb is believed to boost brain power and lift mood by cutting levels of the stress hormone cortisol. Add rosemary sprigs to stews and casseroles, and sprinkle a few leaves over meat, poultry, fish or vegetables before roasting.

Wise up to sage – This strongly flavoured herb boosts brain function – especially memory. Add it to soups, casseroles and stews.

9. Drink plenty of water

Your brain is around 85 per cent water, so even mild dehydration can affect mental wellbeing; psychological symptoms of dehydration include low mood, restlessness and irritability. Experts recommend

1.2–2.2 litres (2–3 pints) of water daily; this may sound like a lot, but remember fruit and vegetables contain a lot of water and can contribute to your daily intake. Tea and coffee can be counted as part of your fluid intake (they still provide some fluid, despite having a slight diuretic effect), but they contain caffeine (see Action 11), so it's best not to drink too much of them.

10. Limit your alcohol intake

A recent UK survey suggested that people suffering from low mood are twice as likely to drink heavily in an attempt to make themselves feel better; unfortunately, drinking excessive amounts of alcohol depletes B vitamins, calcium and magnesium – the very nutrients needed for good mental health and a positive outlook. It's also a diuretic, so it can disrupt your sleep patterns.

The recommended maximum weekly alcohol intake is 14 units for a woman and 21 units for a man. One unit is roughly equal to one small (125 ml) glass of wine, half a pint of beer or lager, one small glass of sherry or port and one single measure of spirits. For more information visit www.drinkaware.co.uk.

11. Cut down on caffeine

Heavy caffeine consumption has been linked to irritability, nervousness, restlessness and insomnia – none of which are conducive to high self-esteem. So if you consume a lot of caffeine-containing drinks and foods like coffee, tea, cola and chocolate, it may be worth cutting down.

The caffeine content of a cup of tea or coffee can vary quite widely depending on the brand, how much tea or coffee is used, how long it's left to brew and, of course, the size of the cup or portion (see the table below). Also, it is hard to say how much caffeine is too much, as some people are more sensitive to it than others – but most experts suggest a daily limit of 300 mg.

Good alternatives to regular tea and coffee include decaffeinated versions, redbush (rooibos) tea, herbal teas and coffee substitutes made from dandelion (e.g. Symington's Dandelion Coffee) or chicory (e.g. Prewett's Instant Chicory). Always wean yourself off caffeine gradually to prevent withdrawal symptoms, which can include headaches and anxiety.

Caffeine in tea, coffee, cocoa and chocolate

Drink/food	Average caffeine content
Tea (mug)	55–140 mg
Instant coffee (cup)	54 mg
Ground coffee (cup)	105 mg
Cocoa (cup)	5 mg
50 g dark chocolate	Up to 50 mg
50 g milk chocolate	25 mg

12. Try mood-boosting supplements

As we've already discussed, low self-worth is often a symptom of depression and low mood, which can be linked to low levels of the neurotransmitter serotonin; taking a serotonin-boosting supplement may help to give both your mood and self-esteem a lift.

Do supplements work?

Often there is only anecdotal evidence that a supplement works. While you need to be cautious about unsupported claims, bear in mind that sometimes the lack of evidence is simply due to the fact that the research hasn't been done. Even though the turnover in the herbal medicine sector is quite high, many manufacturers cannot meet the high financial costs of clinical trials, so a lack of evidence to back up the use of a supplement doesn't necessarily mean it doesn't work or isn't safe – but it is important to exercise caution and make sure you only buy products from reputable companies.

Another problem is that some herbal remedies have several active ingredients and this can make it difficult to identify which produce the beneficial effects. Also, the quality of herbal medicines can vary due to differences in plant species, the type of soil they are grown in, extraction methods and storage, etc. These variations can sometimes make it hard to draw firm conclusions about particular herbs.

It is reassuring to know that the Medicines and Healthcare products Regulatory Agency (MHRA) has recently tightened up the regulation of herbal medicines and supplements to help ensure their effectiveness, safety and quality (see below).

Are supplements safe to use?

It is important to remember that just because something is termed 'natural' it is not necessarily harmless. Vitamins, minerals and herbs contain chemicals that have an effect on the body, just as drugs do. Supplements fall under two categories – herbal medicines and food supplements – and are subject to legislation to help ensure the safety of the people who use them. If you are taking prescribed medications, speak to your GP before taking a supplement to make sure it won't affect their potency or effectiveness, or cause harmful side effects.

Regulation of herbal medicines

According to the MHRA, herbal medicine is any medicinal product that contains one or more herbal substances as active ingredients, or one or more herbal preparations, or a combination of the two. Since April 2011, all herbal medicines have had to be registered under the Traditional Herbal Medicines Registration Scheme, or hold a product licence. Registered herbal medicines have to meet specific safety and quality standards, and carry agreed indications for when and how they should be used. Licensed herbal medicines have to meet certain standards of safety, quality and effectiveness. For more information go to: http://www.mhra.gov.uk/howweregulate/medicines/ herbalmedicinesregulation/registeredtraditionalherbalmedicines/ index.htm.

Regulation of food supplements

Vitamin and mineral products are defined as food supplements and come under the EU Food Supplements Directive. This legislation aims to protect consumers from unsafe products by making sure all supplements are correctly labelled, and only contain permitted amounts of allowed vitamins and minerals. Manufacturers are prohibited from making therapeutic claims about their vitamin and mineral supplements.

Here is an overview of herbal and nutritional supplements that have been shown to help boost serotonin levels. They are available in various forms, including capsules, tablets and tinctures. Related products are listed in the Useful Products section at the end of the book.

> ### Find out more about herbal supplements
>
> MHRA provides a list of herbal products currently registered under the Traditional Herbal Medicines Registration Scheme, along with information sheets on their safe use. You can also report any adverse reactions herbal remedies or supplements may have caused to the agency. The agency's contact details can be found in the Directory at the end of this book.

5-Hydroxytryptophan (5-HTP)

What it is/does: 5-HTP supplements are usually made from the seeds of the Griffonia plant, which comes from West Africa. The body uses 5-HTP to produce serotonin – a lack of which is associated with low mood, anxiety and poor sleep. Several small studies suggest that 5-HTP may be as effective as some anti-depressant drugs for the relief of mild to moderate depression. One study involving 63 people compared the effects of 5-HTP with fluvoxamine (Luvox) – an SSRI (selective serotonin reuptake inhibitor), which is a type of antidepressant that increases the level of serotonin in the blood; those who were given 5-HTP did just as well as those who received Luvox and suffered fewer side effects. In another study, people who took 5-HTP fell asleep more easily and slept more soundly than those who took a placebo.

Safety: 5-HTP should not be taken with SSRI antidepressants such as Prozac, with weight-control drugs, triptans (medication used to treat migraines) or the painkiller tramadol. Nor should it be taken if you are pregnant. Some people may experience a temporary worsening of anxiety symptoms before noticing an improvement.

Available as: Tablets – such as Happy Days 5-HTP, Serotone 5-HTP and Solgar 5 Hydroxytryptophan.

Omega-3 essential fatty acids (EFAs)

What they are/do: Omega-3 EFAs are found in oily fish, nuts, seeds, avocados and seed oils, including rapeseed and flaxseed; if you don't eat these foods regularly taking a supplement may be beneficial. These have several important roles in the brain including enhancing serotonin levels; evidence suggests that the higher your omega-3 levels are the higher your serotonin levels will be.

Safety: Omega-3 EFAs can interact with blood-thinning drugs, such as warfarin. The recommended daily amount for mental wellbeing is 1,000 mg of EPA/DHA (omega-3 fatty acids); both fish oil and cod liver oil are excellent sources of EPA and DHA. Cod liver oil also contains serotonin boosting vitamin D, which many people in the UK are deficient in (because the leading source is sunlight), and vitamin A. However, it is not advisable to take cod liver oil alongside a multivitamin, as any excess vitamin A and D is stored in the liver – too much of these vitamins can be harmful. Alternatively, if you are a vegetarian you could take flaxseed (also known as linseed) oil, which contains ALA from which the body can produce EPA/DHA, but only in small amounts.

Available as: Oil – such as Seven Seas Pure Cod Liver Oil and capsules – such as Seven Seas Pulse Omega-3 Pure Fish Oil. Vertese produces an Omega-3 6 and 9 blend capsule suitable for vegetarians and vegans.

St John's wort

What it is/does: This is a hedgerow plant with yellow flowers. The active ingredient in this herb, hypericin, is thought to keep the chemicals linked to positive mood, such as serotonin and norepinephrine, in the brain for longer by blocking the effects of an enzyme that destroys them.

A 2009 review of 29 studies, involving 5,489 patients with mild to moderate depression that compared treatment with St John's wort extracts for four to 12 weeks with treatment with a placebo, tricyclic, or SSRI antidepressants, concluded the herb was as effective, and had fewer side effects.

Safety: If you are taking any kind of medication, seek advice from your GP or pharmacist before taking St John's wort, as it can react with several commonly prescribed drugs, including the contraceptive pill, anti-epileptic drugs, warfarin and the antibiotic tetracycline. It can enhance the effects of SSRI antidepressants and should not be taken by anyone with bipolar disorder. It can also increase sensitivity to sunlight.

Available as: Tablets – such as Kira Good Mood St John's Wort Extract 450 mg and Nature's Best Pure Grade St John's Wort High Strength One-a-Day, capsules, and as a tincture from suppliers like G Baldwin & Co.

Vitamin B complex

What they are/do: This is a group of vitamins found in meat, fish, dairy products, vegetables and wholegrains. They are involved in several processes affecting the nervous system, including the production of the neurotransmitters serotonin and gamma-aminobutyric acid (GABA), and keeping the blood-sugar levels steady. You could be short of B vitamins if you eat a lot of processed foods, if you're a vegan or if you are under a lot of stress.

Safety: Taking B vitamins is generally safe; but don't take more than 100 mg of vitamin B6 – higher doses can cause nerve damage. If you're pregnant or breastfeeding, suffer from gout, diabetes or liver problems, or have had a stomach ulcer, speak to your GP or pharmacist before taking a vitamin B complex.

Available as: Tablets – such as Solgar Formula Vitamin B-Complex '100' Tablets; and caplets – such as Holland & Barrett Complete B Vitamin B Complex caplets.

Check the benefits

Supplements can take up to three months to have a noticeable effect. If you don't feel your mood and self-esteem have improved by then, consider stopping taking them. If you notice any adverse side effects stop taking them immediately.

Chapter 3

Exercise to Enhance Your Self-Esteem

Research shows that people who take regular exercise have higher self-esteem – probably because they feel more confident about their bodies, and have a sense of pride and achievement.

Exercise also enhances self-esteem by boosting mood and relieving stress; during exercise your body produces the 'happy' hormone serotonin, as well as endorphins, which act like natural tranquilisers. Being active also uses up stress hormones such as adrenaline and cortisol. Furthermore, it takes your mind off the stresses and strains of everyday living, while concentrating on your chosen activity encourages you to live in the present.

Moving around warms and loosens tight muscles, and encourages you to breathe more deeply, which is also calming. Being active also promotes sound sleep because it tires you out physically. Exercising outdoors in daylight also improves sleep quality by suppressing the release of the 'sleep' hormone melatonin, and encouraging the body to produce it at night, as well as having other psychological benefits.

Attending an exercise class or a gym is also a great way to meet people with similar interests; belonging to a social network promotes good emotional health and raises self-esteem.

However, you don't have to go to the gym to lead an active lifestyle; this chapter suggests other easy ways to incorporate exercise into your daily routine. There is an overview of activities including 'green exercise', such as walking, gardening and wild swimming, as well as Pilates, yoga and swimming in an indoor pool.

13. Walk more

Walking is one of the best forms of exercise there is. The health benefits include weight control; a reduced risk of type 2 diabetes, breast, bowel and other cancers; as well as stronger bones and muscles. And, like other types of exercise, walking improves your mental health by triggering the release of the 'happy hormone' serotonin – especially if you walk in a green space.

It's also the cheapest and easiest form of exercise to fit into your daily life; you don't need an expensive gym membership or equipment to do it and it's convenient – you can walk any time, any place and anywhere. You don't even have to travel anywhere to do it – you can start walking the minute you step out of your door!

Even if you work full time it is still possible to fit walking into your daily routine. Here are some ideas to get you started and I'm sure you'll think of more.

- Park your car farther away from your workplace or the shops

- Get off the bus or train one stop earlier

- Park your car on the top level of a multi-storey car park and use the stairs

○ Leave your desk and walk around regularly

○ Use the stairs rather than the lift

○ Take a walk during your lunch break, instead of sitting at your desk

○ Walk to your colleagues' desks to pass on information instead of emailing them

○ Walk to the water dispenser every hour or two for a refill – your brain will benefit from both the exercise and the extra hydration

○ Make trips to the kitchen to make a cup of tea or coffee

○ Walk your dog every day – if you don't have one, offer to walk a neighbour's

14. Take some 'green exercise'

In 2007, research by Essex University for the mental health charity Mind found that taking part in 'green exercise', such as walking or cycling in parks or the countryside, or gardening, made people feel better about themselves, more relaxed and confident.

Following these findings, Mind called for 'green exercise' to be more widely recognised as an effective treatment for mental distress. Studies also show that walking in woodland lowers the blood pressure, heart rate and stress hormone levels, as well as boosting the immune system. Aim to spend some time outdoors in a 'green space' – such as a garden, a park or woodland – each day. Even just a few minutes spent outdoors can be beneficial; further research at Essex University in 2009 suggested that spending just five minutes in a green space significantly boosted mood and self-esteem.

In 2004, research by Japan's National Land Afforestation Promotion found that walking in woodland lowered blood pressure and heart rate, and boosted the immune system. It also reported that people who stopped to admire a pleasant woodland view for 20 minutes had a 13 per cent reduction in the level of the stress hormone cortisol in their bloodstream. The Japanese call this calming, grounding effect of trees *shinrin-yoku*, which means 'forest bathing'.

Experts think these benefits might be down to the higher levels of negative ions near areas with trees and running water. Others think that getting out into green spaces is beneficial because we have a natural affinity with nature and being disconnected from it causes stress and mental health problems. Getting outdoors in daylight even helps you to sleep better because it stops you producing melatonin, the brain chemical that encourages sleep, during the day – making it easier for your body to produce it at night, so you drop off more quickly and sleep more soundly – see Action 26, for further information.

15. Do some gardening

Like walking, gardening is an easy way to fit exercise into your life – even if you don't actually have a garden. You can create your own 'green space' by growing plants and flowers on your balcony or terrace and still enjoy the benefits associated with gardening.

Thirty minutes of gardening can offer the same physical and mental health benefits as a workout – especially if it includes digging. Even light gardening tasks like weeding and watering can improve your strength and agility.

And what could give your self-esteem more of a boost than knowing your beautiful blooms and lush green plants, or delicious fruit or vegetables, are the result of your own hard work?

16. Practise Pilates

Pilates is a programme of low-impact exercises initially developed by a nurse called Joseph H. Pilates to help rehabilitate bed-bound patients. Pilates focuses on teaching you how to pull your pelvic and lower abdominal muscles inwards and upwards. Holding your body in this position during each movement tones the abdominal (core) muscles, and lengthens and strengthens the whole body. It also encourages good posture, which helps to lift your mood and prevent muscular tension and pain, as well as deep, controlled breathing, which helps to relieve stress and leave you feeling grounded.

According to Pilates expert Angie Newson, if you practise Pilates regularly you will feel more energetic and flexible, your posture will improve and you will feel calmer, more relaxed and more able to deal with the stresses of modern-day living. Pilates can be practised at home, as there are various instructional DVDs, online tutorials and apps available, but it is advisable to join a class at first, to make sure you adopt the right posture and perform the exercises properly; most leisure centres and health clubs now offer Pilates classes. The Body Control Pilates Association provides details of qualified instructors (see the Directory at the end of the book).

17. Get in the swim

Swimming is a great way to give your whole body a workout; and, as the Chief Medical Officer's report published in 2004 states, it also has psychological benefits – being in a pool can 'take you away from it all'. This is probably down to having to focus on your breathing, rhythm and stroke, which takes your mind off your worries and encourages you to live in the moment.

Because the body is supported by the water, swimming is accessible to everyone – including people with arthritis, injuries or disabilities – making it a very inclusive form of exercise that is suitable for people who might find other types of exercise too taxing.

Another plus is that every 30 minutes of activity in the pool has the same benefits as 45 minutes of exercise on land, because the pressure and resistance of the water makes your body work harder.

If you visit your local public swimming baths, try to go when it isn't too busy, such as during weekdays or perhaps weekend evenings, to avoid being jostled or interrupted.

Wild swimming in the sea, rivers and lakes is becoming increasingly popular and is especially relaxing because it is another form of 'green exercise'. However, you obviously need to be a competent swimmer. For safety reasons never go wild swimming alone and always do your own risk assessment before you take the plunge. It's also essential that you acclimatise yourself to cold outdoor water, by gradually increasing the amount of time you spend in it. If you're not used to swimming in cold water you can soon find yourself having difficulties – it can quickly numb your hands and hamper your stroke. It's vital that you know how long you can swim comfortably in cold water for and stay within that limit.

To improve your swimming technique either indoors or outside visit www.swimfit.com, a website that offers online coaching programmes.

18. Say 'yes' to yoga

The word 'yoga' comes from the Sanskrit word *yuj*, which means union. Yoga *asanas* (postures) and *pranayama* (breathing exercises) are aimed at uniting the body, mind and soul. Hatha yoga involves stretching the body slowly into the *asanas* and then holding the position; this combination of slow movement and holding poses not only stretches the muscles, but strengthens and loosens them too. It also strengthens the joints and increases flexibility and mobility, which relieves stress and induces calm. The word 'hatha' is derived from the Sanskrit words *ha* meaning 'sun' and *tha* meaning 'moon', and means 'balance'; both the postures and breathing exercises have balancing effects on the body and mind.

Below are just some of the yoga *pranayama* and *asanas* that, with regular practice, could help improve your self-esteem by making you feel better about your body and calming your mind.

Alternate nostril breathing (*nadi shodhana*)
This yoga breathing exercise instils calm and clarity of thought.

1. Using your right thumb press your right nostril closed. Inhale slowly and deeply through your left nostril to a count of four.

2. Hold your breath for as long as you find comfortable. Release your right nostril, then use your right index finger to block your left nostril.

3. Exhale slowly through your right nostril. Next, inhale through your right nostril to a count of four. Hold your breath. Release your left nostril and block the right as you exhale.

4. Complete the cycle five to ten times.

The Mountain Pose (*Tadasana*)

This is a basic standing pose that promotes inner calm and clarity of thought.

1. Inhale, then stand with your feet parallel and slightly apart.

2. Keep your knees straight, and your shoulders and arms loose and relaxed.

3. As you exhale feel your weight through your heels.

The Warrior (*Virabhadrasana*)

This posture encourages you to take up more space and feel 'bigger' and bolder.

1. Inhale, then stand in the Mountain Pose.

2. Exhale, then jump or move your left foot outwards, so your feet are three to four feet apart.

3. Inhaling, turn your left foot about 45 degrees to the right and your right foot about 90 degrees to the right.

4. Exhale, then bend your left knee, ensuring it is directly above your foot, and swivel your torso to the right. Your right leg should be stretched out behind you.

5. Inhale, then with your palms facing inwards and your fingers outstretched, swing your arms above your head and feel the stretch through your right leg and ribcage and up into your arms. Tilt your head back and look up at your hands. Hold for 30 seconds, then exhale and return to the Mountain Pose.

Safe yoga

When practising yoga at home, always proceed slowly and carefully. Wear lightweight, loose clothing that allows you to move freely, and no footwear, as yoga is best performed barefoot. Use a non-slip mat for enhanced comfort, stability and grip. Avoid forcing your body into a posture and always stop if you feel any discomfort. Never do yoga when you have just eaten, or if you feel unwell. Don't try inverted postures if you have a neck or back problem, or have high blood pressure, heart disease or circulatory problems. If you suffer from discomfort after practising a particular posture, stop doing it until the pain has gone. If in doubt, consult your GP.

Chapter 4

Solve Stress for Strong Self-Esteem

A little pressure can be challenging and stimulating, and spur us on to reach our full potential. Without it we'd have nothing to motivate us to get out of bed each morning; most of us would find a life without any kind of pressure boring, and that in itself can be stressful.

However, too much pressure in our lives leads to stress and, left unchecked, stress can cause chemical changes in the body that can eventually lead to health problems – ranging from weight gain, skin conditions, migraines, IBS, aches and pains, colds and flu to depression, high blood pressure, irregular heartbeat and heart disease. Having a poor body image, or suffering from poor physical or mental health, can have a negative impact on self-esteem.

Stress can also cause your self-esteem to plummet, because when you are under excessive pressure you are more likely to feel less sure of yourself and your performance may suffer. This in turn affects your self-image, creating a vicious cycle of poor performance and a negative self-image.

The amount of stress we experience as a nation is growing because our lives are becoming increasingly complex. Modern society is far more aspirational and materialistic than it was, say, 50 years ago. We are faced with a bewildering array of services and products to choose from, and the media and advertisers constantly bombard us with images of the so-called perfect life: slim, attractive people in designer clothes, driving top-of-the-range cars and living in large houses, full of material goods like widescreen televisions and the latest technology. This type of lifestyle is unattainable for most of us, yet the way in which it is portrayed leaves us feeling we must strive to achieve it by working longer and longer hours. Many of us juggle full or part-time work with parenthood, a relationship and running a home, whilst trying to look and feel our best and maintain a social life.

Stress is now the most common reason for British workers to be signed off on long-term sick leave – ahead of back problems, stroke, heart attack, cancer and other mental health issues – and work itself can be a major cause of stress; a report by the Chartered Institute of Personnel and Development in 2011 cited job insecurity caused by the economic downturn, an excessive workload, poor management and restructuring in the workplace as the leading causes of work-related stress.

Other factors involved include lack of control over your work situation, working long hours or shifts, not having time to take breaks, or having too much responsibility. Lack of help and support from your co-workers or supervisors, having no opportunities to advance, and doing a job that is boring and repetitive can also take their toll.

As already mentioned above, many employees are working long hours – often without breaks – hoping to impress their managers and hold on to their jobs. Unfortunately, working in this way is likely to increase your stress levels, which could hamper your performance and make you more susceptible to illness, therefore reducing your productivity.

Psychologists argue that stress arises from your perception of a situation, rather than from the situation itself, so changing the way you view events can help you to reduce stress.

Stress is also a major cause of sleep problems, including difficulty falling asleep and staying asleep. Lack of sleep can trigger the stress response, creating a vicious cycle of stress and insomnia. Too little sleep can also lead to weight gain, low mood and ill health – all of which can have a negative impact on self-esteem.

Clearly, managing your stress levels is an important part of boosting your self-esteem and, interestingly, research suggests that having healthy self-esteem makes you more resilient and able to bounce back after periods of stress. In this chapter we will look at how streamlining your life, managing your finances, reducing work-related pressures, changing how you view challenging situations, taking time out to relax and taking steps to improve your sleep can protect your self-esteem from the stresses and strains of modern-day living.

What are the effects of stress on the mind and body?

Whilst a little pressure can boost immunity, when we are placed under excessive pressure, stress hormones like cortisol have a negative effect on immune function, making us more prone to infections such as colds and flu; allergies such as hay fever, asthma and eczema; and autoimmune disorders such as rheumatoid arthritis. Long-term stress can also cause irritability, depression and anxiety, which can lead to relationship problems and further stress.

As individuals, we are all comfortable with different levels and types of pressure – what is challenging and motivating for one person might be completely overwhelming for another. Also, we all have different reactions to stress – some people suffer from emotional or behavioural symptoms, while others develop physical problems, or a combination of the two. It is important to understand both the difference between pressure and stress, and how much pressure you are able to handle at any one time. It is also vital that you learn to recognise your individual early warning signs and symptoms so that you can take steps to reduce your stress levels before they cause you serious harm.

What is the stress response?

The stress response is how the body responds when confronted with what the brain perceives to be a stressful situation.

The stress response has three stages:

1. **Alarm** – this involves the 'fight or flight' response.

2. **Adaptation** – if the stressful situation isn't resolved, your body uses all of its resources to adapt, and you are likely to suffer from physical and mental symptoms.

3. **Exhaustion** – this is where the body has used up its resources and you are at risk of suffering from more serious health conditions.

Alarm stage

When faced with what you perceive as a stressful situation, the sympathetic nervous system takes over to trigger the alarm stage of the stress response. This is designed to enable us to deal with difficult, or even dangerous, situations and involves the brain preparing the body to either stay put to face the perceived threat, or to escape from it. This worked well in primitive times when you might have to deal with a passing threat or danger fairly quickly, but unfortunately the situations that induce the stress response (stressors) nowadays are unlikely to require either of these responses, and can happen more often and go on for longer. The 'fight or flight' response triggered at the alarm stage induces the following reactions in the body:

- Adrenal glands release stress hormones cortisol and noradrenaline, from which the body produces adrenaline

- Heart rate speeds up

- Liver releases energy stored as glycogen

- Blood sugar rises

- Cholesterol level rises

- Blood pressure rises

- Breathing becomes faster and shallower

- Sweating increases

- Blood vessels close

- Digestion slows down or speeds up

- More white blood cells are released, increasing immune function

- Fibrin, a substance that promotes blood clotting, is released into the bloodstream

You may notice these physical signs of acute stress:

◯ Forehead tenses

◯ Eyes strain

◯ Jaws and teeth clench

◯ Skin tightens

◯ Mouth dries up

◯ Feelings of anger or hostility

Adaptation

Your body is under strain as it harnesses its resources to adapt to chronic stress. During this stage the body continues to produce stress hormones to provide energy to deal with the situation. Stress hormones affect the way the immune system functions – increasing your risk of infections, autoimmune and allergic conditions. Over time the effects of this stage of the stress response include:

Physical

◯ Sleep problems

◯ Tiredness

◯ Muscular aches and pains, especially in the neck, shoulders and back

◯ Headaches or migraines

☐ Irritable bowel syndrome (IBS)

☐ Indigestion

☐ Skin conditions, e.g. eczema or psoriasis

☐ Asthma

☐ Allergies

☐ Food intolerances

☐ Weight gain or loss

☐ Fewer white blood cells released

☐ Minor infections, e.g. colds or sore throats, due to reduced immunity

☐ Palpitations

☐ Menstrual changes

☐ Loss of libido

Mental

☐ Difficulty making decisions

☐ Poor performance

- Lack of concentration

- Forgetfulness

- Panic attacks

- Becoming more emotional

- Self-blame

- Feeling inadequate

- Dwelling on the past

- Worry

- Inability to relax

- Feeling tense and anxious

- Impatience

- Irritability

- Losing your temper easily

- Tearfulness

- Poor sense of humour

Behavioural

- Recklessness

- Smoking more

- Drinking more alcohol

- Using recreational drugs

- Poor appetite or overeating

- Craving sugary, fatty or salty foods

- Talking too quickly

- Outbursts of anger

- Avoiding contact with other people

- Nervous habits, e.g. nail biting, hair pulling, fist clenching, foot tapping, blinking and nervous tics

Exhaustion

The body has used up its physical and emotional resources. Relentless bombardment from stress hormones over a long period of time has reduced levels of important brain chemicals, impaired immune function, raised blood pressure and cholesterol levels, and increased blood clotting, leaving the body at risk of more serious health problems. These can include the following:

- Depression

- High blood pressure

- Irregular heartbeat (arrhythmia)

- Obesity

- Coronary heart disease

Clearly, stress can have a serious negative impact on your physical and mental health, therefore managing it should be considered an integral part of working on raising your self-esteem. This chapter aims to help you both reduce the amount of stress you experience and relieve the effects of stress.

19. Streamline your life

Prioritise

When you feel overwhelmed by the number of tasks you need to do at home or at work, make a 'to-do list'; now identify the three most important tasks you must do today and make sure you do these first. If you have time to complete anything else that will be a bonus.

Identify which activities you can do less often, or even stop doing altogether, to make more time for the things that are most important to you. Say 'no' to non-essential tasks you don't have time for, or just don't want to do. It's a little word, but it can have a big effect on your stress levels.

Tackle a two-minute task

If there's a task on your to-do list that will only take two minutes, for example making a quick telephone call, answering a short email or paying a bill, do it as soon as you have a couple of spare minutes – and feel in control.

Delegate

Don't feel that you have to shoulder responsibility for every task. If you share a house with others, make sure everyone does their fair share of the chores. Discuss who should do what and, if necessary, draw up a weekly rota and stick it on the fridge or in another prominent spot.

De-clutter

A jam-packed wardrobe, heaving shelves and overflowing cupboards can raise stress levels as you struggle to find things. De-cluttering your home can save you time and energy, leave you feeling calmer and more in control, and can even improve your finances.

If you have a lot of things to sort through, enlist the help of your partner, a family member or a friend, if you can, or try tackling one room at a time. First sort items into two piles – the things you want to keep and the things you don't. If you're a hoarder and can't bear to part with things, apply the two-year rule – if you haven't worn, read or used an item for two years or more put it into one of three piles: 'bin-it', 'donate to charity', or 'recycle or sell it'; you can recycle goods through Freegle, Freecycle or Clothes for Cash (see Directory). You can also sell them on sites like eBay for a small fee. Bigwardrobe. com is website that allows you to swap or sell unwanted clothes; free membership allows you to swap one item per month, or for a small yearly membership fee you can swap as often as you like, as well as buy or sell items. Don't forget to sort through your toiletries and cosmetics. Dig out products that have been pushed to the back of the bathroom cupboard and, if they are still within their use-by date, either vow to use them before you buy more, throw them out or take them down to your local charity shop.

De-cluttering can be hard work, but the results are worthwhile; not only will you feel a sense of achievement, but you may also have helped a worthwhile cause or boosted your bank balance. But, most importantly, you'll be amazed at how much more at ease you feel when your house is clutter-free.

Try this: If you can't bear to part with an item, store it under a bed or in the loft. Make a rule that if you haven't wanted to use it or wear it within a year, you will get rid of it.

Tips for a tidy home

Once you've cleared the clutter, try these tips to stop it from building up again:

1. Keep a waste bin in every room

2. Recycle newspapers and letters you don't need to keep as soon as you have read them

3. Ensure you have plenty of cupboards, boxes and shelves for storage

4. Ask everyone in the house to tidy up after themselves

5. Use up existing toiletries, cosmetics, cleaning products, etc. before buying new ones

6. De-clutter at least once a year

Take the stress out of cleaning

◯ To make cleaning the house less stressful, only tackle a couple of rooms at a time

◯ Clean first, then vacuum

◯ Clean the dirtiest room first

◯ Wear an apron with pockets, so that you can keep your cleaning products, cloths and dusters close at hand

◯ Clean from left to right, top to bottom and from the back of an item to the front – without doubling back

◯ Only clean dirty areas, i.e. don't clean a whole door – just wipe away any visible marks

20. Avoid information overload

We live in an age where there is a constant stream of information directed at us through TV, radio, print media, texts, emails, the Internet and social media sites like Twitter and Facebook; this means our brains are continuously stimulated with images, facts and ideas that they have to make sense of. Psychologists have termed this 'infomania'.

In 2005, research carried out at the Institute of Psychiatry, London, suggested that the effects of constant texting and emailing throughout the day on the brain's functioning are akin to those caused by losing a night's sleep. If your brain is constantly 'on standby' waiting for the next message or piece of information, it can affect your productivity as it can only deal with one thing at a time. It can even lower your IQ; the researchers found that constant emailing and text messaging lowered mental capability by an average of 10 points in an IQ test.

Television

TV can be addictive: the more programmes you watch, the more you want to watch. There are more TV channels and programmes available than ever before and news is broadcast 24/7, so it is tempting to have the television on all the time. While watching TV can be relaxing, entertaining and informative, too much can crowd out other enjoyable and enriching activities, such as talking to your partner and children, socialising with friends, reading a book or doing something creative such as painting, knitting or other crafts. TV also tends to promote the materialism and perfectionism that lead to stress and self-criticism.

Try this: Be selective about your TV viewing – choose the programmes that really interest you and either watch them live, on a catch-up service such as BBC iPlayer or 4OD, or record them to view later. Switch the television off when there is nothing you really want to watch and do something else with your precious time.

Texting

Texting is a great way to communicate with people quickly and easily, but sending, receiving and responding to dozens of texts a day can not only interrupt your concentration at work, but also your ability to 'switch off' and relax at home. Not only that, research at the University of California found that texting while you're doing something else – like watching TV or surfing the Internet – simply overloads the brain and affects your ability to absorb information. Over-reliance on texting can also have a negative effect on relationships and friendships if it replaces face-to-face or telephone conversations.

Try this: Have text-free areas at home; for example, make it a rule not to text at the dining table, or in the bedroom; when you need to concentrate on one task, or want to wind down before bed, switch your mobile phone off.

Email

Reading and responding to emails can eat up a lot of time; how often have you read all of the emails in your inbox for another dozen or more to appear within minutes? Many personal emails are unsolicited junk mail or offers from online companies we have previously bought items from, and sometimes it is hard to resist opening them just in case they are offering us the deal of a lifetime.

Try this: Only check your personal emails a couple of times a day. Ensure the spam filter is always on and, if any junk emails slip through, discipline yourself to delete them without opening them. As soon as you have answered an email either file it away in a folder or delete it.

Email Overload ?

A 2011 survey by the UK-based work management company Mindjet, reported that British workers receive an average of 36 emails each day.

Internet

The Internet is a great source of information and entertainment, but if you find yourself surfing for hours on end, you could be frittering away time that could be spent following other interests. It is also very easy to get hooked on Internet shopping, and before you know it you have a hefty credit card bill for stuff you don't need and little time left for real life! Twitter, Facebook, LinkedIn and other social networking sites are free and can be useful, so long as you don't spend hours and hours of your spare time using them rather than meeting your friends and family members face to face.

Try this: Set yourself a daily time limit for online browsing and aim to stick to it. Only answer the Twitter or Facebook messages you want to respond to. Use the time you save to do the things you always feel you don't have time for.

21. Take control of your finances

Overspending and debt can be both a cause and effect of low self-esteem. When you don't feel good about yourself you might be tempted to go out and buy things you don't really need to make yourself feel better; this can lead to spiralling debts and leave you feeling even worse about yourself, creating a cycle of low self-esteem and debt. Debt is a major source of stress in today's materialistic times; in 2008, an online survey of more than 1,400 people in the UK by the Really Worried website found that the number-one concern was the cost of living, closely followed by energy prices, debt and pensions.

Reassessing how you spend your hard-earned cash and taking control of your finances can help you to break free from the low self-esteem and increasing debt cycle, as well as reduce your risk of financial problems and suffering from the stress they can cause. If you feel that low self-esteem is behind your overspending, your first step towards managing your money better is to work on raising your self-esteem by following the tips in this book. Once you have improved your self-worth, you should find it easier to manage your money wisely so that it enables you to live your life the way you want, whether that means spending more time with your family, going on holiday or even changing jobs, cutting the number of hours you work or retiring.

Set and stick to a realistic budget

Work out how much money you need to cover your essential outgoings, such as food, mortgage or rent, gas, electricity, insurance and travel, then set yourself a realistic budget and stick to it. Check to see if you can save money by switching your mortgage lender or energy supplier; paying your bills by direct debit will usually get you the cheapest deal. Keep a spending diary in which you record every item you buy for a month. You will soon spot where you are frittering away your hard-earned cash, and then you can start taking control of your finances and making sure that you only buy the things you really want and need.

Check your direct debits and standing orders to see if you're paying for something you don't use or need, for example, insurance on goods you no longer have, a subscription to a magazine you never get around to reading, a gym membership you never use, or an 'added value' bank account that you pay an extra fee for only to find you don't use the additional benefits, such as mobile phone insurance or credit card protection. Once you've identified your money wasters, cancel them.

Pay off any debts as soon as possible. If you are struggling to meet credit card or mortgage payments, always speak to your lender as soon as you possibly can and try to negotiate an amount you can manage to pay. Pay off the debts with the highest interest rates first. If you are in serious debt through credit and store cards you need to take drastic action – cut them up now!

If your main purpose in life is the pursuit of material goods, you could find that you have to work longer and longer hours to earn enough money to pay for them, and you are becoming more and more stressed in the process.

Spend your money on your priorities

Rather than spending your money on things you don't really need or want simply to meet social expectations, or to make yourself feel better, think about what is most important to you in your life and then spend your money accordingly. For example, if you enjoy going on holiday a couple of times a year, maybe you could direct more of your money towards the costs of your travel by cutting out another major expense, such as running a car; if your local public transport services are adequate or if you could cycle or walk to work, do you really need one?

Live more frugally

If your wardrobe is crammed with clothes, half of which you never wear, perhaps it's time to stop and think before you buy the latest fashion must-have. If you see something you like, go home and think about it before you buy. Ask yourself: do I need it? Will I wear it? Does it suit me? Can I buy it somewhere else for less? If you decide it's something you really need you can go back later to buy it. Once you've bought a garment, leave the labels on until you've had a chance to try it on again at home. You may find that you've changed your mind about it; most shops allow you to return unworn clothing with the labels still intact up to 28 days after you bought them, and if it takes you even longer to make up your mind, selling clothing with tags still attached on sites like eBay is likely to earn you more money than without.

If you tend to buy the most expensive brands of cosmetics and perfumes, you could try buying cheaper ones; surveys often show that cheaper products give as good, or even better, results than their more expensive counterparts. When you buy more expensive brands you are often paying for their higher advertising and packaging costs.

If you spend a lot of money on eating out you could limit it to a weekly treat and make the most of local 'early-bird' deals. Eating at your local college restaurant – the food is usually reasonably priced and of high quality – and checking daily deals sites for money-saving vouchers for local eateries are other ways of cutting the cost of eating out.

If you enjoy reading, make use of your local library or swap books with friends once you have read them. Alternatively, register with a book-swapping website such as www.readitswapit.co.uk. You could also take part in a scheme called BookCrossing, which enables you to find, share and track books. To find out more go to www.bookcrossing.com.

Check online for the cheapest holiday deals – all-inclusive deals tend to be the most cost-effective as you don't have to worry about how much you'll spend on eating, drinking and entertainment once you reach your destination.

Focus on rewarding activities that cost little or nothing – anything from walking in your local park to going to free concerts, or visiting free art galleries and museums – so long as you enjoy it and it helps you concentrate on 'being' rather than 'having'.

Cut your food bills

Food is the cornerstone of good health but is becoming ever more expensive. Work out how much you can afford to spend on nourishing yourself and your family, and then aim to buy the foods that form a healthy balanced diet (see Chapter 3). Plan your meals for the week ahead, then make a list of the foods you need before you go shopping and stick to it.

If you're on a tight budget, focus on meals made from cheap but nutritious ingredients, such as fruit and vegetables, pulses, potatoes, brown rice, wholemeal bread, whole wheat cereals, pasta and oats. Eggs, baked beans, tinned sardines and tuna are all economical sources of protein and other nutrients. These foods can form the basis of family meals such as stir-fries, broths, casseroles and pasta dishes. You can save money on basic foodstuffs by looking for the 'value' brands at major supermarkets, buying at budget supermarkets, or by buying in bulk – for example, by taking advantage of 'buy one get one free' or other special offers. Compare food prices at different supermarkets. My Supermarket is an online supermarket that enables you to compare prices and shop online from the main UK retailers in one place – go to www.mysupermarket.co.uk.

Keep a lookout for foods that are priced down because they are close to their sell-by date. You can often buy fruit, vegetables and meats more cheaply at your local market – especially at the end of the day or on a Saturday.

Make your own cheaper and healthier versions of ready meals by cooking extra portions of your favourite dishes and freezing them.

Grow your own vegetables; it could save you a lot of money and you will reap the health benefits of eating produce that is not only pesticide-free, but also fresher than that bought in the supermarket. You don't need a large garden or an allotment – you can grow a variety of vegetables, including potatoes, carrots, peas, tomatoes, beetroot and broad, French and runner beans in pots or containers. Use a deep pot or container and put stones or pieces of broken pots in the bottom for drainage, then fill with compost (grow-bags tend to be cheaper) before planting and watering.

Take a home-made sandwich, soup or salad, plus fruit and yogurt, to work for lunch. It is far healthier and cheaper than buying lunch. If you give up that daily takeaway cappuccino, too, you could save as much as £100 each month.

Living more frugally will enable you to spend less, but still afford the things you enjoy.

Get the savings habit

A 2012 survey of 2,000 people for National Savings and Investments found that making regular savings boosted people's mood and gave them a sense of achievement, so squirrel away some of the money you've saved into a savings account. If you are a tax payer, an ISA will give you the best interest because it isn't taxed, otherwise check current rates on a money comparison site like www.moneysupermarket.com.

22. Cut work-related stress

Try the following steps to make your working day less pressured and help you avoid, or at least reduce, work-related stress.

Get ready for work

Preparing for work the night before by getting your clothes and any work equipment ready, helps to get your working day off to a stress-free start. If you find it hard to decide what to wear, try having a particular outfit for every day of the week, so that you don't even have to think about it. Plan what you will eat for breakfast and prepare your packed lunch to save time in the morning. If you have children you could also get their school uniforms, school bags and packed lunches ready for a much calmer start to the working day.

Customise your workspace

To avoid tension in your body, perfect your posture by adjusting your work area. If you work with a computer screen it should be straight ahead, so you don't have to twist your neck, shoulders or torso. You should be able to see the screen sitting upright, not leaning forwards or backwards. The top of the screen should be in line with your eyes. Your upper arms should be at your sides and your wrists and forearms should be horizontal when you use your keyboard. Adjust your seat height if necessary. Your pelvis should be slightly higher than your knees. Your feet should be flat on the floor – if you can't manage this, use a shallow footrest. If you're not sure if your workspace is suitable for you, ask your employer to check it complies with health and safety regulations.

Green your desk

Research at Washington State University in 2011 claimed that having a plant on your desk at work can cut stress levels, lower blood pressure and boost productivity. These benefits are thought to be down to the calming, air-purifying and humidifying effects of plants. Foliage plants are thought to work better than flowering plants because they produce the most oxygen.

Tidy your desk

Keeping your desk tidy makes it easier to concentrate on your task in hand. Sort through any paperwork and decide what to do with it; if it needs to be acted on put it in your in-tray to be dealt with as soon as possible; if you will need it at a later date, file it away where you can find it easily; if it is out of date, or no longer needed, bin it or recycle it.

Clear your desktop

Once a month clear the desktop on your computer of files and icons that you no longer use. By deleting unused files you will keep your desktop clean, organised and easier to use, as well as free up memory space, helping your computer to work more quickly and efficiently.

Manage your workload

Managing your workload will not only reduce the amount of stress you experience at work but also improve your performance – which will in turn boost your self-esteem.

Write a to-do list at the end of your working day, in preparation for the next day. If you have a long to-do list, number tasks in terms of urgency and importance, then carry them out in that order. Cross off tasks as soon as you complete them.

If you have a few telephone calls to make, letters to write or emails to respond to, try 'chunking'. Chunking is where you set aside a period of time to complete similar tasks together.

Avoid 'catching' stress

According to Professor Elaine Hatfield, a psychologist from the University of Hawaii, stress in the workplace can be contagious – if a colleague is stressed you can unconsciously 'absorb' their negative emotions. To avoid 'catching' stress when a colleague is complaining about their work or personal life, try saying something positive about their situation, or offer to help them. If they persist in being negative try taking a break – perhaps by going to make a cup of tea. If you can't walk away, make a determined effort to stay positive and avoid adopting your colleague's mindset.

Take a break

No matter how busy you are you should make time for one or two short breaks during your working day. Going for a walk, or even just reading a newspaper – preferably away from your desk – can take your mind off work and lower your stress levels.

Socialise

While too many interruptions from emails, phone calls, text messages and colleagues chatting can lead to work piling up, being sociable at work has been shown to reduce stress. So take five minutes for a cuppa and a chat, if you can, during your working day.

Deskercise

Stretching your body every hour or two helps to loosen the muscles and get the blood flowing, helping to prevent blood clots. It can also improve your productivity and mood; exercise increases blood flow to the brain, boosting brain power and memory, and stimulates the release of mood-lifting endorphins. Focusing on something other than your computer screen also helps to prevent eye strain. Even just walking to the kitchen, or going to the photocopier can help. If you don't have time to leave your desk, try these 'deskercises' from your chair.

- Clench your calf and thigh muscles, hold, then release. Repeat two or three times.

- Lift and tense both shoulders and hold for ten seconds. Allow them to drop and relax. Repeat three times.

- Circle each shoulder alternately two or three times – first forwards and then backwards.

Place the backs of your hands on your lower back. Arch your back by pushing your hips forward and pulling your shoulders back. Hold for ten seconds and repeat up to three times.

Stretch both arms out in front of you at shoulder height, palms upright. Bend your forearms back and touch your shoulders with your fingertips. Repeat up to five times.

Clench your fists tightly for five seconds. Stretch your fingers out then relax them. Repeat up to five times.

Switch off!

Switch off from work after hours by turning off your mobile phone or BlackBerry, and avoiding checking your emails. If you have to bring your work things home with you, put them away so that they stay out of sight and out of mind. Changing out of your work clothes into leisure wear also helps you to mentally separate your working life from your home life.

23. Practise mindfulness

As you walk, eat and travel, be where you are. Otherwise you will miss most of your life.   Buddha

When we are children most of us find it easy to live in the present, because we aren't burdened by the past and haven't yet started worrying about the future. As a result, we can enjoy life as it happens minute by minute. However, once we become adults and take on more and more responsibilities, most of us start pondering over our past and worrying about what might happen in the future, both of which increase stress levels unnecessarily.

Enjoy your life now

It's much easier to deal with everyday life when you focus on the 'here and now', because you can give your full attention to what you are doing; it's hard to focus on the task at hand when you are busy worrying about the past or the future.

Research by the US National Academy of Science suggested that living in the present, also known as mindfulness, reduced stress levels and boosted the immune system.

When you live in the present your life is more enjoyable and less stressful, because instead of doing things on autopilot, all of your senses are focused on what you're doing and what is going on around you. For example, imagine going for a walk in a beautiful park while being so preoccupied with worries about the future, or regrets about the past, that you don't even look at your surroundings. Now picture yourself on the same walk, but this time stopping to take in the beauty of the plants and trees around you, listening to the birdsong and breathing in the scents, and think how much more pleasurable and relaxing it would be.

On a more practical level, if you focus on your current task at work, instead of worrying about other jobs you need to do, you will probably find you complete it more quickly and efficiently. If you don't have a lot of time to spend with your family, focusing all of your attention on them when you are together, rather than thinking about, or doing, other things at the same time, will be far more rewarding.

Living in the present is a skill that can be learned. Don't worry if you find it hard at first – whenever your mind starts wandering bring it 'back' to the present. Yoga requires concentrating on your breathing and your body as you do different postures, and is a good example of living in the moment. Taking part in a sport or doing something you find engrossing, like cooking a meal, painting a picture, knitting or sewing, can also keep your mind firmly in the here and now.

Keeping a daily diary might help too, because it encourages you to think about what is happening in your life right now.

Try this:

◗ Start by focusing on your breathing – be aware of the rise and fall of your chest as you breathe in and out.

◗ Notice any tension in your body – tighten the affected muscle, then let it relax.

◗ If you're eating, concentrate on the sight, smell, taste and texture of your food – don't watch TV or read at the same time.

◗ If you're having a conversation, actively listen to what the other person is saying, instead of letting your mind wander.

◗ If you're doing a chore like washing up or ironing, focus fully on what you are doing.

◗ If you're having a shower, feel the pressure and warmth of the water on your skin and smell the aroma of the soap or shower gel you are using.

◗ If you go outdoors, use all of your senses to absorb the sights, sounds and smells around you as you walk.

Avoid worrying about the future

Unease, anxiety, tension, stress, worry – all types of fear – are caused by too much future, and not enough presence.

Eckhart Tolle, *The Power of Now*

Living in the present means you can use your energy to deal with real situations, rather than wasting it worrying about events that haven't yet and may never happen; so rather than agonising over what could go wrong at a forthcoming event, such as a meeting, job interview or exam, take practical steps to prepare for it, so that you feel more confident and in control. If you feel daunted by the size of a task, rather than worrying about it, break it down into small, achievable steps.

Being mindful also involves not trying to forecast the future; how often have you thought of the worst possible outcome to a current situation and then found a few days, weeks or months later things turned out far better than you imagined and all of that angst was completely unnecessary?

Not only that, the body's stress response cannot differentiate between what is real and what is imaginary. For example, if you worry about being made redundant and being unable to pay the mortgage, your body will release stress hormones, even if you keep your job.

It's hard not to think about what could go wrong in your life, but it's better for your mental health if you can make a conscious effort not to worry about things that may never happen. It's also important to accept that not everything in life is easy and to put things in perspective.

Try this: List some situations you've worried about in the past. Next to each one write the outcome you feared most. Now mark each outcome with a tick or a cross according to whether or not it actually happened.

You should find that:

a) The outcome you feared most didn't materialise.

or

b) Things actually turned out far better than you imagined.

or

c) Even if your worst-case scenario did come to pass, you dealt with it, eventually came to terms with it and learned from it, then moved on.

For more information on mindfulness take a look at the Mental Health Foundation's Be Mindful campaign at www.bemindful.co.uk.

24. Change your perception of a situation

Cognitive behavioural therapy (CBT) is a type of psychotherapy that focuses on removing the negative thoughts and unhelpful behaviours that can lead to emotional problems, including stress. According to cognitive theory many of us develop negative beliefs about ourselves as a result of our experiences during childhood and early adulthood, for example, being bullied at school, parents divorcing, failing an exam, etc., and that these take root in our minds until they become automatic. Behavioural theory is based on the belief that behaviour is a learned response that is also a reaction to past experiences. CBT is based on a combination of both types of theory.

According to CBT an event or situation is only stressful if you think it is, because your feelings aren't facts – they are just your perception of an event or situation and your ability to deal with it.

Count your blessings

Research suggests that people who notice and express gratitude for the good things in their lives tend to be happier and more optimistic than those who complain about the things they lack. Count your blessings by listing all the positive things in your life. Whenever you are feeling negative revisit your list and try to add to it.

How you perceive and react to events in your life is down to the filters you view them through. These filters include your personality, values, beliefs and attitudes, which have been shaped by your genetics, upbringing, past experiences, lifestyle and culture. So it is possible to cut the amount of stress you feel about a situation simply by changing your perception of it and your ability to handle it.

Try the ABC approach next time you're feeling stressed:

Activator – write down the situation that is making you feel stressed, for example, a forthcoming job interview.

Beliefs – note down your thoughts about the situation and your ability to cope with it, for example, 'I hate interviews'. 'I can never think of good answers to questions in a job interview'.

Consequences of A and B – record your feelings and actions, for example, worried, apprehensive.

☐ **D**ispute your negative thoughts – think of more positive ways of viewing the situation, for example, 'I've been successful at interviews before – even when I didn't think they had gone very well'; 'I really want this job, so I am going to do the best I can at the interview'.

☐ **E**ffective new approaches – choose new, helpful thoughts and behaviours, for example, 'I'll prepare for the interview by researching the company and practising interview techniques with my partner'.

If you follow this formula each time you face a stressful situation, you will gradually create a more positive image of yourself and your ability to cope with what life throws at you. Your new self-belief will enable you to identify effective solutions to problems and reduce the amount of stress you experience.

25. Meditate

Meditation is a form of mindfulness as it involves focusing your mind on a particular activity, thought or object and disregarding any distractions. Clinical studies show that meditating regularly induces deep physical and mental relaxation and reverses the adverse effects of stress. As well as reducing stress levels, meditation can encourage positive thinking and a more positive self-image.

Below are four different types of meditation: the first involves focusing on your breathing; the second involves visualising a relaxing retreat; the third involves focusing on a word or phrase (mantra);

and the fourth involves tensing and then releasing your muscles, as you breathe in and out.

1. Simple breathing meditation

With every breath we take, oxygen is absorbed into the blood to produce the energy we need for every function in our bodies. When we're stressed our breathing tends to be fast and shallow, which leads to a drop in the level of calming carbon dioxide in our bloodstream. This can make us even more stressed and cause muscular tension in the neck, shoulders and upper back. Slow, deep breathing decreases the heart rate, increases production of calming alpha brainwaves, relaxes the muscles, relieves tension, and triggers the release of 'happy hormones' serotonin and dopamine.

Focusing on your breathing also helps take your mind off your worries and is a simple form of meditation. So the next time you're feeling stressed or anxious, take control of your breathing.

1. Ensure you are sitting or lying comfortably.

2. Close your eyes and start focusing on your breathing.

3. Breathe in slowly and deeply through your nose to a count of five, allowing your stomach to expand. Hold for five seconds.

4. Exhale slowly for ten seconds, as you gradually pull your stomach in.

5. Whenever a passing thought distracts you, simply return to focusing on your breathing.

2. Visualise your favourite retreat

Visualisation allows you to escape from everyday stresses and strains, and can be done whenever you have a few spare minutes. When you vividly imagine a pleasant scene your mind responds by producing the same endorphins and other pleasure-giving chemicals it would if you were actually there.

1. Find a comfortable place to sit or lie and close your eyes.

2. Focus on breathing in and out deeply, as in the previous exercise.

3. Next imagine your favourite retreat, for example, a woodland with tall green pine trees and a gently flowing stream, or maybe a beach with white sand, blue skies, turquoise sea and lush palm trees.

4. Now use all of your senses to vividly imagine your retreat; smell the scent of the pine trees, hear the gentle hiss of flowing water, feel the heat of the sun on your face and body, and hear the crash and roar of the waves.

5. Enjoy the scene until you feel ready to return to reality.

6. Breathe in and out slowly and deeply. When you are ready, open your eyes.

3. Mantra meditation
A mantra is a word or phrase that you use to induce a state of relaxation. Using a mantra to help you relax is another form of meditation. A 2012 study at the Medical College of Wisconsin, involving 201 participants with an average age of 59 years, found that participants practising this form of meditation for 20 minutes twice daily had reduced stress and blood pressure levels and were 48 per cent less likely to have a heart attack, stroke, or die from all causes, compared with participants who attended a health education class across a period of over five years.

Try this mantra exercise to help you relax:

1. Choose a word or phrase that suggests relaxation to you such as: 'Peace'; 'Calm'; 'I am relaxed'; 'My muscles are relaxing'.

2. Sit quietly and shut your eyes.

3. Breathe in and out slowly and deeply, as in the previous two exercises.

4. Repeat your mantra out loud or in your head, on each out-breath.

5. If your mind wanders, simply bring it back to the mantra, repeating it with more emphasis.

4. Muscle relaxation

Whenever you feel stressed you're likely to tense your muscles, which will no doubt make you feel even more stressed. When you release the tension from your muscles you naturally feel more relaxed.

Try this muscle relaxation sequence before or after other meditations, or whenever you are feeling tense.

1. Inhale deeply through your nose, then tense the muscles in your face by clenching your jaw and screwing up your eyes tightly. Release the muscles in your face as you exhale through your mouth.

2. Take a deep breath in through your nose, then lift your shoulder muscles, tense them for a few seconds and then allow them to fall, releasing the tension as you breathe out through your mouth.

3. Inhale deeply through your nose, then clench your fists and tighten the muscles in your arms, hold for a few seconds, then release and exhale through your mouth.

4. Next, breathe in through your nose, tense the muscles in your buttocks and legs, hold, then relax them as you breathe out through your mouth.

5. Finally, breathe in through your nose, clench your toes and tense your feet, hold, then release them as you breathe out.

Obviously, it isn't always convenient to follow the above sequence when you are out and about. Below is a speedy muscle relaxation technique you can practise discreetly anytime, anywhere, without people noticing.

> ### Speedy relaxer
>
> ☐ Take a deep breath in through your nose, tightening up your shoulder and back muscles. Hold for five seconds.
> ☐ Breathe out through your mouth slowly, allowing your shoulders to fall and the muscles to relax.
> ☐ Imagine all of the tension drifting out of your body.

26. Sleep more soundly

Stress is a major cause of sleep problems, because feeling tense or worried makes it hard to fall asleep and stay asleep. Lack of good quality sleep is a major stressor because during sleep part of the brain processes and stores information, while the brain cortex rests and recovers. Also, the body repairs tissue wear and tear and produces growth and appetite-regulating hormones, as well as disease-fighting white blood cells. After just one night of poor sleep we are less able to cope with pressure and are more likely to be suffering from low mood and irritability, have problems concentrating and remembering things, and succumb to infections and illness – all of which can contribute to a vicious cycle of stress and insomnia.

According to a 2011 survey of 5,300 people by Mental Health Matters, poor sleepers are also four times more likely to experience relationship problems and are twice as likely to suffer from fatigue. Lack of sleep is also linked to weight gain, as it lowers levels of the appetite-controlling hormone leptin. Also, research at the Karolinska Institute in Stockholm in 2010 suggested there is such a thing as 'beauty sleep'; a study found that volunteers were judged less attractive and healthy looking after a night with little or broken sleep compared with when they had a normal night's sleep. Feeling physically or mentally below par, or feeling overweight, or unattractive could have a hugely negative impact on your self-esteem, so making sure you sleep well is vital. Try these tips to ensure you sleep soundly.

Get outdoors in daylight to halt the production of melatonin, the brain chemical that promotes sleep; this makes it easier for your body to release it at night, so you fall asleep more quickly and sleep more soundly. Blue light, which is light from a blue sky on a clear day, is believed to be the most beneficial.

Eat foods rich in tryptophan, an amino acid from which your body produces first serotonin and then the 'sleep' hormone melatonin. Tryptophan-rich foods include chicken, turkey, bananas, dates, rice, oats, whole grain breads, cereals and dairy foods, which also contain calming calcium, hence a glass of warm milk at bedtime can be very effective for helping you sleep.

Make sure you're neither hungry nor over-full when you go to bed, as both can lead to wakefulness; ideally, avoid eating a heavy meal later than two hours before bed. However, if you are hungry at bedtime, a light snack such as oatcakes and cheese, or a turkey sandwich, could help you to sleep more soundly.

Avoid drinking coffee or cola, or eating chocolate after 4 p.m. – the caffeine in them can have a stimulant effect for hours. Although tea contains about half the caffeine – around 50 mg per cup – it's best to avoid drinking it near bedtime if you have trouble sleeping. Drink redbush (rooibos) or herbal teas, which are caffeine-free, instead.

Exercise before 8 p.m.; this raises your body temperature and metabolism, which fall a few hours later, triggering sleepiness. Taking exercise any later could cause wakefulness, as your body temperature might still be raised at bedtime. Lack of physical activity, however, can lead to restlessness and difficulty sleeping.

Wind down before bedtime. Develop your own evening routine that lets you 'put the day to bed'. This might include watching TV – if you find it helps you relax – but avoid anything that might prey on your mind later when you're trying to fall asleep and aim at switching the TV off half an hour before bed. Many people find reading or listening to music helps them to unwind.

Dim the lights to encourage your body to release sleep-inducing melatonin – a dimmer switch, lamp, or candles are ideal for this.

Soak in a warm bath before bed. Your temperature rises with the heat and then falls, promoting sleep. The warmth can also help ease muscular and mental tension, especially if you add relaxing essential oils like lavender or chamomile.

Avoid drinking alcohol at bedtime. It might help you relax and drop off more quickly, but it also disrupts sleep patterns, meaning you have less deep sleep. It is also a diuretic, so you are more likely to wake up to make trips to the toilet during the night.

If keeping away from alcohol doesn't help you sleep better, try a glass of wine made from grape skins that are especially rich in melatonin, such as Cabernet Sauvignon, Merlot or Chianti.

Make your bedroom as inviting and relaxing as you can with fresh bedding and soft lighting, to make bedtime a pleasure.

Keep your bedroom cool. Your brain attempts to lower your body temperature at night to slow down your metabolism and encourage sleep; around 18°C is ideal.

Hang dark, heavy curtains or black-out blinds, or wear an eye mask, to block out the light. Darkness stimulates the pineal gland in the brain to produce melatonin.

◯ Cut down noise from traffic or your partner's snoring by wearing earplugs.

◯ Check your mattress gives you the right level of support; lie on your back then slip a hand under your lower back. There should be just enough space to fit your hand in the gap between your back and the mattress. If you can't, the mattress is too soft for you. A bed board under the mattress might help. If the gap is bigger than this, the mattress is too hard.

◯ Pick a pillow that holds your spine in line with your neck. The best pillow thickness for you depends on the width of your shoulders – if you have narrow shoulders choose a flatter pillow; if you are broad-shouldered, you might need two pillows. Memory-foam pillows are another good choice, as they mould to your shape to support the head and neck.

◯ Banish TVs, computers, iPads and mobile phones to help your brain associate your bedroom with sleep and sex only. Watching TV or using a computer or other technology last thing at night can over-stimulate your brain, making it hard to switch off and fall asleep. Screens also give off bright light, which can hamper melatonin production.

◯ Clear your mind of worries about problems or events happening the next day by jotting down your concerns or a plan for the day ahead before going to bed.

◯ If you still feel tense at bedtime you could try one of the meditation techniques outlined in Action 25.

If you wake during the night and start dwelling on problems, try telling yourself firmly: 'You can't do anything about this now, so go to sleep and think about it tomorrow'.

Only go to bed when you feel sleepy. If you don't drop off within about 20 minutes, get up and do something you find relaxing, like reading or listening to soothing music. Only return to bed when you feel drowsy, to help your brain associate your bed with sleep.

Finally, if you have trouble falling or staying asleep try not to worry, as this will make you even more stressed and less likely to drop off; instead remind yourself that research suggests most people underestimate how much sleep they have had and can lose a few hours now and again without suffering too many problems. With a more relaxed outlook you may even find yourself sleeping better!

Chapter 5

Accept Yourself

We live in a society of high expectations in terms of what we should achieve in our careers, our appearance and our personal lives. Though aiming to achieve your full potential is positive, it is important to make sure it is *your* full potential and not someone else's. The media constantly bombard us with images of impossibly beautiful people, wearing designer clothes, living in expensive, immaculate houses and driving top-of-the-range cars. If you can't achieve these ideals it's easy to start feeling that you're somehow not good enough and this can have a hugely negative impact on your self-esteem. Also, if you have low self-esteem it's likely that you will ignore or downplay your strong points, thus perpetuating your negative self-image.

In this chapter we look at how you can avoid perfectionism and comparing yourself to others, and accept and approve of yourself as you are. We discuss how healthy self-esteem comes from self-knowledge and self-acceptance, which involves identifying your values and carrying out an honest appraisal of your strengths, talents and achievements, as well as accepting the way you look and making the most of your appearance.

Once you know what makes you tick, you can take steps to ensure that your life reflects who you really are. This involves doing what you want to do, not what someone else, or society, expects, as well as using and developing your personal qualities and natural abilities.

When you focus on doing the things that matter most to you and that you excel at you are more likely to enjoy life and achieve success, which in turn will increase your self-esteem. Reminding yourself of past achievements can also help to boost your self-belief and spur you on to do well in the future – again helping to build self-esteem. True self-esteem comes from giving yourself credit where it's due, rather than simply telling yourself you're great, regardless of how you behave or perform.

Being able to ask for what you want and encourage others to treat you with the respect you deserve also raises self-esteem, so you will find tips on how to be more assertive at the end of this chapter.

27. Stop trying to be perfect

Trying to achieve a so-called perfect life could mean you put unnecessary pressure on yourself; whether that means constantly cleaning to keep your house pristine; always dieting to achieve the perfect body; or running up debts to buy clothes and other material goods that you don't really need. Having unrealistic expectations of yourself can chip away at your self-esteem; for example, trying to be the 'perfect' mother might mean you beat yourself up if you find you can't manage to breast feed; failing to achieve the 'perfect' body might mean you can never relax around food or feel happy with your body shape and appearance. It's easy to fall into the trap of thinking you can only be a worthy person if you improve yourself or your life in some way, so you start thinking: 'I'll be happy with myself when I've lost weight/ got my dream job/met a new partner/bought a better car/bought a new house.' Whilst it's good to have aspirations and goals – achieving them can boost your self-esteem – it's important to acknowledge and be happy with what you have already achieved.

Tell yourself 'I'm doing the best I can'

Telling yourself that you're doing the best you can in every area of your life and learning to accept that you and your life are never going to be perfect is one of the best ways of repairing low self-esteem caused by perfectionism. Going back to the examples on page 93 – the mother berating herself for not being able to breast feed could tell herself that whilst breast milk offers many health benefits to both mother and baby, being a good mother is more about the amount of unconditional love you give to your child than the type of milk you provide them with; the person who is unhappy with how they look might consider that the media images showing celebrities with perfect skin and enviable figures have probably only been achieved after spending hours with a make-up artist and extensive airbrushing and that none of them look that way in real life.

Try this: Next time you start comparing yourself unfavourably to others remind yourself that you are unique – there is no one else in the world exactly like you; no one else has the personality traits, talents, skills and experiences that combine to make you who you are. No one else can make the same contribution you make to the world.

28. Learn to love the way you look

Feeling happy with the way you look is a source of high self-esteem. However, problems can arise when you rely on your appearance more than anything else for your feelings of self-worth, as this can lead to an obsession with your body image that could eventually develop into an eating disorder, or a desire to make drastic changes to your face and body with cosmetic surgery. Also, when your looks change with age, your self-esteem could drop dramatically unless you value other aspects of yourself equally. It is much healthier to view your appearance as just one component of your attractiveness and self-worth, along with your positive character traits, talents and abilities – beauty really is more than skin deep.

Remember too that what you see when you look in the mirror is coloured by your self-esteem and mood at the time; when you're feeling low you might focus on a blemish or other imperfection that other people probably won't even notice. Many very attractive people in the media confess to having low self-esteem. How they appear to other people and what they perceive when they look at their reflection are often completely different. How happy you are with your appearance has a lot to do with how you feel about yourself overall. If you work on improving your self-esteem in general, so that you don't judge yourself solely on your looks, you should find that you feel less concerned about any perceived imperfections. This is not to say that you shouldn't make the most of your looks – we all feel better about ourselves when we know we are looking our best, and taking care of your appearance is an outward sign of high self-esteem; but avoid trying to emulate the unrealistic, artificially constructed ideals portrayed by the media.

The key to looking your best is not to try to look the same as someone else, but to make the most of your best features and play down your less attractive ones. It means accepting that if you are only five feet tall you are never going to look like a willowy catwalk model, or if you have wiry, curly hair you are never going to have long, silky tresses – but that doesn't mean you can't look great. As we've already mentioned in Chapter 2 and 3, eating well and taking regular exercise will help ensure your body looks good – whatever size or shape you are – and your hair and skin will be in tip-top condition too. Whether you are a man or a woman you can then perfect your appearance with good grooming. Take good care of your hair and skin. Get the best haircut and colour you can afford. Have regular manicures – you can save money by doing your own. Choose clothes that flatter your size and shape and reflect your personal taste and style. Once you know you are looking your best you can forget about your appearance and concentrate on enjoying your life and being the best you can be in other areas.

29. Be yourself

Being yourself means living your life in a way that reflects who you really are. It involves focusing on what is important to you whilst using and developing your unique strengths and talents, rather than doing things to please others or to conform to society's expectations. This might sound self-centred, but psychologists report that the more authentic people are, the happier and more fulfilled they are likely to feel. Not allowing yourself to be who you really are can lead to stress, unhappiness and low self-esteem – all of which will have a negative impact not only on you, but on the lives of people around you. Quite simply, if you feel content and fulfilled you will be much more pleasant to spend time with.

Many of us spend our lives trying to be someone we're not, for example, by doing a job we don't enjoy because it pays well or it sounds impressive. Life is too short to spend it doing things you don't enjoy. For example, if you love being outdoors, sitting at a desk in a stuffy office for 40 hours a week is probably not the best career choice; if you feel at your happiest when you are with other people, working alone at home wouldn't suit you. Being yourself involves making life choices that reflect your values and passions, and utilise your particular strengths and talents. Rather than trying to change who you are, aim to be the best version of yourself you possibly can.

Although it's great to have role models who inspire you, avoid trying to be like someone else; if you think of successful people like the singer Adele, entrepreneur Richard Branson and actress Helen Mirren, you will realise that they have become great by capitalising on their unique strengths, talents and personalities, not by trying to be the same as everyone else. When you make the most of your natural abilities and strengths you are more likely to be successful, which in turn creates strong self-esteem.

30. Live your values

Your values are the things that are most important to you; often we are so busy earning a living, running a home, etc. that we lose sight of what matters most to us. When you live according to your values you will feel a sense of purpose, fulfilment and contentment. Also, your life will be more balanced because you won't be neglecting the areas that are most important to you in favour of things that are less so. In short, living your values will increase your overall happiness, and when you feel happy you can't help but feel better about yourself. If you're not sure what your values are, start by writing down everything that is important to you. This might include one or more of the following, as well as priorities that you identify for yourself:

- Family

- Relationships

- Friendships

- [ ] Health

- [ ] Spirituality

- [ ] Nature

- [ ] Pets

- [ ] Money

- [ ] Career

- [ ] Fame

- [ ] Success

- [ ] Independence

- [ ] Travel

- [ ] Adventure

- [ ] Freedom

Once you have a list of values, pick out the five that are the most important to you. These are your core values.

Now check whether you are living by your core values. If you are not, perhaps you could start thinking of the steps you can take to ensure that you get to do the things that matter most to you. For example, if your family is one of the areas of your life that you value most, but you work full-time and spend your weekends catching up with chores, so you don't get to spend much quality time with them, think of ways to change this. You could cut the number of hours you work (if you can afford to) or ask family members to help with the chores, so that you have more time to spend with them. If wildlife and nature are important to you, perhaps you could join a local, national or even international wildlife protection group, such as the Wildlife Trusts, the Animal Protection Agency or Greenpeace. If you don't prioritise the things that matter most, you can end up drifting along in life feeling unfulfilled and frustrated. Life is too short to live it on autopilot.

31. Identify your strengths

These are your positive character traits. Identifying your personal strengths will help to increase your self-esteem in two ways; firstly, it will help you create a more positive view of yourself. Secondly, it will help you to make choices in life that play to your strengths, so that you are more likely to achieve success.

Try this: Write down your major life events or achievements and next to each one note down the personal strengths you feel you have demonstrated within each of these situations.

The following list might give you some ideas:

- Kindness

- Empathy

- Loyalty

- Courage

☐ Fairness

☐ Honesty

☐ Optimism

☐ Persistence

☐ Creativity

☐ Curiosity

☐ Communication

☐ Modesty

☐ Vitality

☐ Open-mindedness

☐ Forgiveness

☐ Leadership

☐ Organisation

☐ Teamwork

32. Play to your strengths

Now that you have identified your strengths, ask yourself: do I play to my personal strengths at work and at home?

If your answer is 'no', try to identify ways you could make better use of your strengths. For example, if you consider yourself to be creative but don't get the opportunity to use this skill in your job, maybe you could take up a creative hobby such as drawing, knitting or woodwork. If you're good at organising, perhaps you could take on an organisational role at home, for example, managing the household budget, arranging holidays, writing the shopping list, etc. You could also use your organisational skills at work by setting and meeting deadlines, initiating ideas, delegating tasks and arranging meetings, or by finding a job that requires these sorts of skills.

If you find it difficult to recognise your strengths, ask your partner, a family member or a friend you trust which positive qualities they have noticed in you.

33. Recognise and use your talents

Your talents are the tasks and activities you are naturally good at. People who have risen to the top of their chosen fields have done so by focusing on their innate talents and becoming the best version of themselves they possibly can be. Good examples include J. K. Rowling, Jamie Oliver, Rihanna, David Beckham, Gary Barlow and Jessica Ennis.

Identifying, using and developing your natural abilities enables you to shine; you can then achieve more and be successful, which in turn feeds your self-esteem.

Everyone has at least one latent talent. Perhaps you are unusually good at mental arithmetic, writing, languages, public speaking, teaching, cookery, gardening, interior design, singing or acting? Or maybe you excel at sports, playing a musical instrument, or arts and crafts? If you can find the time to do the things you are really good at you are more likely to fulfil your potential, and increase your self-esteem and happiness in the process.

As a college tutor delivering a self-esteem-boosting programme, I asked students to write down ten things they were good at. Some students produced a list in minutes and talked about their abilities with pride; others identified a few talents, while others struggled to think of any. This may have been partly because in our society it's considered boastful to tell people you're good at something – even though acknowledging your talents is one of the best ways of building authentic self-esteem – but for many it was down to being led to believe by both parents and teachers that they weren't capable of much.

The response of a painting and decorating student with dyslexia sticks in my mind; he sat for a long time looking at a blank page. When I quizzed him, he replied: 'But I'm not good at anything.' After much prompting he eventually conceded: 'I suppose I must be good at painting and decorating – I got a good report from my tutor.' Women who were hoping to return to work after taking career breaks to look after their family struggled with the task too; it was only when I asked them if they'd successfully raised a family and run a home that they realised they had many transferable skills and talents to draw upon in the world of work.

Now try listing your top ten talents:

1. ....

2. ....

3. ....

4. ....

5. ....

6. ....

7. ....

8. ....

9. ....

10. ....

If you find it difficult, try this:

1. List anything you do well without trying too hard. The tasks you learn quickly and can do almost effortlessly are the ones you have an innate talent for.

2. Now write down your passions. What do you love to do? What excites and inspires you?

3. Finally, study both lists and pick out any common activities; these are the areas you are most likely to excel in and gain fulfilment from. Now that you have identified where your natural abilities lie, check whether you are using and developing them – either at work or at home.

If your answer is 'no', start looking for ways you could use and develop your talents. For example, if you are great at baking cakes you might like to make and sell cupcakes in your spare time. If you are good at gardening you might decide to run an allotment in your spare time and perhaps sell some of your produce. Developing your skills and making money in the process is a great way of building your self-worth.

These might sound like obvious choices, but it's surprising how many people spend their lives doing jobs they don't particularly enjoy and allow their spare time to be taken up with chores or passive pastimes like watching TV, when they could be doing the things they have a passion for and excel at. If you are naturally good at something, you might eventually find a way to develop it from a hobby or sideline into a full-time career. You will find advice on setting and achieving goals to help you improve your skills and achieve your dreams in Chapter 7.

34. Acknowledge your achievements

This is a sure-fire way to build your self-esteem and to motivate yourself to do well in the future. In the course of day-to-day living it's easy to forget the things you have done well in the past; focusing on the achievements you are most proud of can help you build up your self-esteem, especially if it's recently taken a knock.

Try this: List your top ten achievements.

1. ....

2. ....

3. ....

4. ....

5. ....

6. ....

7. ....

8. ....

9. ....

10. ....

If you're struggling to think of ten achievements, you're not alone – many of my past students couldn't think of any, initially. However, when they looked back over their lives in more detail they soon realised that many of the things they had forgotten about, or dismissed as unimportant, were achievements they could be proud of. Accomplishments they identified that might help you think of your own included: 'Winning a football trophy'; 'Coming top in Science'; 'Getting a degree'; 'Bringing up my children well'; 'Getting a good job'; 'Passing my driving test'; and 'Buying and doing up my own home'.

Whenever you are feeling unsure of yourself and your abilities, look at the list you have made and feel a sense of pride in what you have achieved. Better still, add a new achievement to your list if you can!

35. Encourage others to treat you with respect

It's likely that your new self-awareness will mean that you want to express your desires and needs to others more effectively; when your self-esteem is low it's likely that you:

Agree with other people's beliefs and opinions to avoid hurting or upsetting them, or to gain their approval, because you lack the confidence to say what you are really feeling.

⬜ Allow people to talk you into doing things you don't really want to do because you lack the confidence to say 'no'.

To give you some idea of what being assertive means, below is the 'Assertiveness Bill of Rights'; believing that you have these rights indicates strong self-worth.

Assertiveness Bill of Rights

1. I have the right to express my feelings.
2. I have the right to express my beliefs and opinions.
3. I have the right to say 'no'.
4. I have the right to change my mind.
5. I have the right to say 'I don't understand'.
6. I have the right to be myself.
7. I have the right to decline responsibility for other people's problems.
8. I have the right to make reasonable requests of other people.
9. I have the right to set my own priorities.
10. I have the right to be listened to.

Learning how to be more assertive will enable you to say what you want, feel and need, and to stand up for your rights, calmly and confidently, without being aggressive or hurting other people's feelings. This will encourage others to treat you with more respect, which will help to improve your self-worth.

The following tactics will help you to express your emotions and stay in control of your life, doing things because you want to, rather than to please other people.

- Choose the right time and place to talk.

- Make eye contact but don't stare, as the other person may find this unnerving.

- Speak calmly, clearly and firmly, but avoid shouting.

- Be clear in your mind about what you want to say before you speak.

- Aim to be concise and to the point, rather than rambling.

- Take responsibility for your own thoughts, feelings and behaviour by saying 'I' rather than 'we', 'you' or 'it'. Rather than saying 'You make me angry', try something like 'I feel angry when you... ' This is less critical and antagonistic to the other person.

- When you can choose whether or not to do something, say 'I won't' or 'I am not' instead of 'I can't' to demonstrate that you've made an active decision, rather than making it sound as though something, or someone, has stopped you. Use 'I want to' instead of 'I have to', and 'I could', rather than 'I should', to show you have a choice. For example: 'I am not going out tonight' or 'I could go out tonight, but I want to stay in', instead of 'I can't go out tonight'.

If you think your feelings or needs aren't being considered, use the 'broken-record' technique: state what you want calmly, repeating it until the other person demonstrates they've heard and understood what you've said; respond to legitimate points raised by the other person, but ignore comments or criticisms that aren't relevant. Avoid getting irritated, loud or angry, as you could come across as aggressive and antagonistic.

When making a request, say exactly what you want using positive, assertive phrases, like those outlined above. For example, if you want to ask someone to help you tidy the house you might say: 'I'd really appreciate it if you could empty all the wastepaper bins.'

Give the other person the opportunity to respond to your comments or requests.

When you have more than one point to make, pause before the next one, so that the other person has a chance to digest each piece of information.

When refusing a request, state why without apologising. For example: 'I'm not coming to see you today, because I've been really busy at work all week and feel really tired.'

If you disagree with someone, say so using the word 'I'. Explain why you disagree, but acknowledge the other person's right to have an opposing viewpoint. For example: 'I don't think I'm being selfish by wanting to stay in today, but I know you look forward to my visits so I can understand why you think that.'

Once you start acting more assertively you should find that people respect you more for being honest and open with them. It is also better for your mental and physical wellbeing if you express how you feel, rather than bottling up negative emotions. Furthermore, it is beneficial for your relationships, as sometimes people bottle things up until they reach breaking point and then end up saying things they regret, or get really upset.

Chapter 6

Use the Power of Positive Self-Talk

In Chapter 4 we looked at CBT and how it is based on the theory that your feelings aren't facts – they are your perception of an event or situation – and that you can change your behaviour by changing your thoughts.

In this chapter we are going to continue this theme by looking at how your self-talk – which is another name for your thoughts – affects your self-esteem. Self-talk is often used to describe the continuous internal dialogue we have with ourselves day in, day out. It is estimated that around 50,000 thoughts pass through our minds every day. If your thoughts about yourself and your experiences are mainly positive you are likely to have high self-esteem; if you tend to talk about yourself critically in your mind you are more likely to have low self-esteem. If you have high self-esteem you are more likely to do well in life and, as a result, think well of yourself; if you have low self-esteem you may not achieve your full potential and this will perpetuate your poor opinion of yourself.

So your thoughts (self-talk) affect how you feel about yourself (your self-esteem and self-image), which in turn affect your actions (your achievements), which come full circle to affect your thoughts again. This is the self-talk cycle. For high self-esteem you need to focus on your positive traits and talents, rather than on your shortcomings, and think about yourself positively. This will help you to improve your performance and level of achievement, which will increase your self-esteem.

This chapter shows you how to challenge any negative thoughts you have about yourself and replace them with more realistic and positive ones, so that you develop a higher opinion of yourself.

Self-concept

Your self-concept is basically how you perceive and evaluate yourself. How you perceive yourself is your self-image; how you evaluate yourself is your self-esteem. Your self-talk feeds your self-image as well as your self-esteem. Without even being aware of it, your subconscious mind has stored away an image of who you are and what you are capable of achieving based on all the attitudes and opinions about yourself that you've taken on board throughout your life. Your subconscious mind then makes sure you act exactly how you imagine yourself to be. For example, if you see yourself as being hopeless at maths, you will perform badly in maths tests, or at doing everyday mental arithmetic; if you tell yourself 'I hate meeting new people', you will act in a way that bears this out and avoid social gatherings. Even if you do something that disproves your beliefs, such as doing well in a maths test, or making a new friend, you will discount this because it doesn't fit in with your current perception of yourself and simply revert back to your 'normal' behaviour.

36. Break the negative self-talk cycle

To break the negative self-talk cycle you need to challenge the critical comments you make about and to yourself, and replace them with more positive, but realistic ones. Remember your thoughts aren't facts; they are simply your perception of the truth.

Keep a daily diary

For a week, note down all the negative and critical comments you make to and about yourself. Then challenge these negative statements by looking for evidence that they may not be true. You might be surprised by how many things you've done well that you've simply dismissed because they don't match your current self-image.

Finally, you are going to construct more positive and realistic statements about yourself which will boost your self-belief. You might find it helpful to refer to your lists of strengths (Action 31), talents (Action 33) and achievements (Action 34).

37. Choose positive self-talk

1. **Choose a negative statement you have recorded in your diary.** For example, 'I never achieve much at work'.

2. **Now look for evidence that challenges this statement.** For example, 'My manager told me I was a valued member of the team at the last team meeting' or 'My paperwork is up to date'.

3. **Finally, write down more positive statements based on this new evidence.** For example, 'I'm a valued member of the team' or 'I meet my targets at work.'

Do this systematically with each negative thought about yourself and then vow to use the new positive statements rather than the old negative ones from now on. Accept and take on board compliments from other people, rather than dismissing them. All of this will build a positive self-image and strong self-esteem, which will make you even more competent and in turn promote positive self-talk.

Case study, Susan, 54

Susan is a college tutor. She was a bright pupil who passed her eleven plus and went to grammar school. Whilst there, she did well in English, French, chemistry and Latin. She did well in maths at junior school but she started telling herself that she couldn't do maths after she couldn't answer a mental arithmetic question in class and her teacher told her she should have known the answer. After that her marks went down and she failed her maths O-level. Later in life she went back to college and then on to university where she had to study statistics as part of the course's research methods module. She believed everyone else was better than her at maths and, as a result, lagged behind in class. When the maths exam loomed she told everyone she didn't think she would pass. Then one of her fellow students said: 'Why don't you look at it as a challenge?' She decided to do just that and spent the next few weeks going over the formulae she had learned during the module. She took the exam and told me: 'I was amazed when the research methods tutor stopped me in the corridor and told me that I had got the best mark in the class – 83 per cent – for my statistics paper!'

This case study demonstrates the power of self-talk; Susan did well in the exam because she stopped telling herself: 'I can't do maths' and focused instead on proving that she could.

Spend time with positive, supportive people

Avoid spending time with people who put you down and make you feel bad about yourself. If someone you know seems to take pleasure in finding fault with you or the things you do it might be time to distance yourself from them. People who really care about you should be positive and supportive. If you can't avoid these people – for example, because they are family members or work colleagues – deflect their negative comments by telling yourself they are only their opinions, not the truth.

Chapter 7

Aspire and Achieve

With your new self-knowledge and a more positive view of yourself and your abilities, you are now ready to set goals that reflect what you want out of life. Working towards meaningful goals will give you a sense of purpose; achieving them will give you a sense of pride and increase your overall feelings of competence. This will give you a much more solid foundation on which to build healthy self-esteem than by simply telling yourself 'I'm great'.

This chapter aims to help you choose specific goals that matter to you, so that you feel motivated to achieve them by taking appropriate actions. You will learn how to break your goals down into achievable first steps and regular success habits (the long-term daily/weekly/monthly actions you need to take), so that you can track and acknowledge your progress and greatly increase your chances of success. We all know that in real life it isn't always easy to stick to our plans, no matter how determined we are, so there is a section on identifying possible obstacles and devising solutions before you start working towards your goals. You'll discover how to utilise the power of your subconscious mind to help you achieve your goals by creating and using effective affirmations. Fear can often stop people from doing the things they want to do, so we end the chapter by looking at how you can overcome your fears and break out of your comfort zone to achieve your dreams.

38. Work out what you want in life

What do you want to be, do and have? Choose goals that inspire, excite you and fit in with the values, strengths and talents you identified in Chapter 5. Think about each area of your life, for example, family, relationships, friendships, social life, career, finance, health and fitness, spirituality, fun or adventure and write down what they would look like in your ideal life.

Don't do something to please someone else, or because you feel that you have to – choose something that you really want to do, that you feel passionate about – then you'll have the motivation to keep going until you achieve your aim.

39. Set SMART goals

To increase your chances of success each goal should be:

Specific – state exactly what you want
Measurable – can be measured, so that you will know when you have achieved it
Ambitious – your goal should stretch you
Realistic – you should truly believe you can achieve it
Timed – set a deadline, but be prepared to extend it if you have to. The most important thing is that you continue to work towards your target until you reach it.

Examples

Weight loss
Vague goals: 'To lose weight'; 'To be slim'.

SMART goals: 'To lose 1lb each week for the next 14 weeks'; 'To wear a size 12 dress at the office Christmas party'.

Financial security
Vague goals: 'To save money regularly'; 'To be able to live comfortably'.
SMART goals: 'To save £50 every month'; 'To earn £40,000 next year'.

40. Plan to achieve

It is vital that you make a written plan of your goals. When you write down what you want to achieve and why, you are more likely to commit to it mentally. It also enables you to work out how and when you will achieve your goal and allows you to track your progress.

Key points to consider

Why do you want it?
Why do you want to achieve your goal? What benefits will seeing it through to the end bring you? These will be your reward for all of the hard work you put in and will keep you motivated when the going gets tough.

How will you do it?
To achieve anything in life you must take action. The easiest way to reach any goal is to break it down into simple, attainable steps. With most goals there will be a few initial steps you need to take to start you off on the road towards achieving your goal. In your goal plan you will list these steps and record when you achieve them; this will boost your self-esteem and spur you on to success.

Examples

Goal: To save £50 every month

First steps:
1. Keep a spending diary to identify what I spend my money on
2. Work out how I can save money
3. Create a budget I can stick to

Goal: To lose 1lb each week for the next 14 weeks.

First steps:
1. Buy or borrow a book about nutrition
2. Collect healthy recipes
3. Plan how I will fit more exercise into my daily routine

41. Identify your success habits

Most goals are achieved and maintained by taking new long-term actions that you repeat daily/weekly/monthly until they become a habit. Think of top Olympic athletes; they didn't achieve a gold medal after a week's intense training. They would have trained every day, month in, month out, until it became a habit. Research suggests that the secret to winning in any athletic sport is to devise a training routine and stick to it, no matter what. The same applies to achieving any goal; taking the above examples, you are more likely to lose weight and keep it off by adopting long-term modest changes to your eating and exercise habits than by going on a short-term drastic diet or exercise routine that you will find impossible to stick to. You are more likely to achieve financial security by becoming a habitual saver than by investing in a get-rich-quick scheme. When it comes to achieving goals it really is the little things you do every day that bring success. So think of the new habits you would need to adopt in order to succeed.

Examples

Goal: To lose 1lb each week for the next 14 weeks

Daily success habits:
1. Avoid snacking and eat more fruit and vegetables
2. Go for a 20-minute walk during my lunch break

Weekly success habits:
1. Plan healthy meals for the week ahead and write a shopping list
2. Weigh myself once each week and record my weight and any weight loss

Monthly success habits:
1. Check how much weight I have lost over the past month
2. Reward myself for sticking to my plan with a non-food treat, for example, a massage, or a new perfume or beauty product

Goal: To save £50 every month

Daily success habits:
1. Take my own packed lunch to work
2. Make coffee at work instead of buying a cappuccino at the cafe
3. Keep an accurate record of my spending

Weekly success habits:

1. Only buy what I really need when I go shopping

2. Calculate my weekly spending and plan to cut back where necessary

Monthly success habits:

1. Review my monthly spending to check if I have stuck to my budget and, if not, identify where and how I could make improvements

2. If I have stuck to my budget reward myself with an inexpensive treat

42. Find solutions to obstacles

You might now be thinking: 'All of this sounds great and looks really good on paper, but things are never that easy in real life, are they? What if I can't stick to my plans for some reason? What will I do then – just give up?'

Achieving a goal requires resilience. Resilience is essentially the ability to bounce back after obstacles or setbacks, and take positive action to resolve issues, rather than simply giving up and abandoning your goal. The best way to overcome obstacles is to identify some you might encounter and possible solutions before you start, that way you can prevent, or be prepared for, things that might go wrong.

Bear in mind, though, that sometimes things might happen that are beyond your control and you can't prepare for, for example, you might hurt your back and have difficulty going for a walk every day, or you might lose your job so you can't keep on saving £50 every month. Remember, most goals aren't achieved overnight – they are usually the result of sticking to regular habits – so falling by the wayside now and again won't stop you from achieving your goal in the long term, so long as you return to your regular success habits as soon as you can. Instead of berating yourself, use positive self-talk like: 'I've done really well to get this far. One mistake or setback isn't going to stop me from succeeding.'

Example

Goal: To lose 1lb each week for the next 14 weeks

Obstacles:

1. My partner always cooks my meals and serves large portions which I feel I have to eat

2. I haven't got time to go to the gym

Solutions:

1. Suggest healthy recipes for my partner to cook and ask if I can serve my own portion

2. Fit exercise like housework, walking and gardening into my daily routine

43. Affirm and succeed

In the last chapter we talked about how your subconscious makes sure that you act in a way that matches your self-image, and that by changing your self-talk you can change your self-image and self-belief. You can use this concept to help you reach your goals by affirming that you have already achieved them. An affirmation is a positive written statement about yourself that you repeat again and again, until your subconscious mind accepts it as the truth and you start acting in ways that make it a reality.

An effective affirmation should be:

1. **Personal** – because you can't change anyone's thoughts or behaviour but your own, so always include the word 'I'.

2. **Positive** – remember, how you think affects how you act, so focus on what you want to achieve, not on what you don't want.

3. **Present tense** – as though it is happening now.

4. **Achievement-oriented** – use phrases like 'I have', 'I do', 'I am', 'I can'.

5. **Emotional** – describing how you will feel when you reach your goal will make it feel more real for example, 'happy', 'confident' 'relaxed', 'energetic'.

6. **Realistic** – can you imagine yourself achieving it?

So, if your goal is to lose a stone in weight, some effective affirmations might be:

- 'I am slim, happy and healthy.'

- 'I enjoy eating healthy food.'

- 'I feel confident and energetic because I exercise every day.'

- 'I am now a stone lighter, and I look and feel great!'

Seeing is believing

A goal is nothing more than a dream with a deadline

Joe L. Griffith

There's a reason we describe our goals as dreams; most of us imagine ourselves achieving them before we take steps to make them a reality. When you do this, you are changing your self-image and paving the way for your subconscious to make sure your actions move you towards this new picture of yourself.

So, to make your affirmation more effective you need to visualise the image your words create. Words create pictures, sounds and emotions.

Try this: To imprint your affirmation on your subconscious mind, read it out loud first. Now close your eyes and picture yourself experiencing your goal in detail, using as many of your senses as possible. How do you look, walk and talk, now that you have reached your goal? How do you feel? Proud? Confident? Happy? Feel the emotions you have attached to your goal. What can you hear? Hear your friends and family congratulating you; they might say, 'Well done' or 'Congratulations', 'I knew you could do it'. Reading, picturing, feeling and hearing your affirmation will have a powerful effect on your subconscious mind. Your subconscious won't accept an affirmation overnight – repeat each affirmation as often as you can until your mind accepts it as reality – you should soon find yourself adopting behaviours that support your new self-image.

Sample goal plan

Now let's put all of these steps together to see what a completed goal plan would look like:

Goal: To lose one stone in 14 weeks
Why I want to achieve it: To look and feel better
Benefits:
1. I will be able to wear a size 12 little black dress at the next work Christmas party

2. I will feel fitter and healthier

Obstacles	Solutions
Overeating when I'm bored.	Find some new interests.
Comfort eating.	Talk through my problems with someone I trust.
Eating out.	Choose salad as a starter or side dish. Avoid foods in batter and creamy sauces.

First steps:
1. Read a book about nutrition
2. Collect healthy recipes

Daily success habits:
1. Walk to work every day
2. Only eat at mealtimes

Weekly success habits:
1. Weigh myself once per week to check my progress
2. Go for a long walk every Sunday afternoon

Monthly success habits:
1. Calculate my weight loss for the past month
2. Reward myself for any weight loss with a non-food treat

Deadline: 15 December.

Affirmation 1: 'I am slim, healthy, happy and brimming with energy.'
Affirmation 2: 'I'm at my work Christmas party and everyone is telling me I look fantastic in my size-12 little black dress.'

Blank goal plan (for your use)

Goal:

Why I want to achieve it:

Benefits:

1. ....

2. ....

3. ....

Obstacles	Solutions

First steps:

1. ....

2. ....

3. ....

Daily success habits:

1. ....

2. ....

3. ....

Weekly success habits:

1. ....

2. ....

3. ....

Monthly success habits:

1. ....

2. ....

3. ....

Deadline: ....

Affirmation 1: ....

....

Affirmation 2: ....

....

44. Don't let fear stop you from taking that first step

Fear can be paralysing and can prevent us from taking that first step towards a goal. Many of us stay in our comfort zone rather than confronting our fears. According to Susan Jeffers, author of *Feel the Fear and do it Anyway*, it is no good waiting until the fear goes away before you take that first step – because it never will!

She says the only way to lose your fear is to go out and do whatever it is you are afraid of doing, and that it's the same for everyone, even the people you think are really confident. So if you're afraid of learning to drive, book that first lesson; if you're scared of going to college to learn a new skill, enrol on that course. Eventually you will lose your fear, before moving on to the next challenge you find scary. If you stay stuck in your comfort zone rather than taking a risk, you will always be afraid. Doing things when you are frightened of doing them requires courage, but the payoff is that you get to expand your horizons and improve your self-esteem. The good news is that if you use affirmations regularly you will be mentally practising the things you fear, so that you are more likely to feel safe when you step out of your comfort zone.

Chapter 8

Get the Feel-Good Factor with DIY Complementary Therapies

Complementary therapies (sometimes known as alternative, natural or holistic therapies) aim to treat the whole person, as opposed to conventional Western medicine, which only treats the symptoms of ill-health, not the individual. More and more people, worried about the side effects of prescribed drugs, are turning to complementary therapies to improve their general physical and mental wellbeing, or to help them manage chronic health conditions.

Complementary therapists see illness as a sign that physical and mental wellbeing have been disrupted, and attempt to restore good health by stimulating the body's innate self-healing and self-regulating abilities. They believe that total wellbeing comes from the mind, body and spirit being in a state of balance called homeostasis.

Homeostasis can be achieved by following the type of lifestyle recommended in this book; a wholesome diet with plenty of fresh air, exercise, rest, relaxation and sleep, combined with stress management and a positive mental attitude. Complementary therapies such as aromatherapy, massage and reflexology can help you to achieve homeostasis by reducing stress levels, easing pain, promoting relaxation and improving sleep.

Whether complementary therapies work or not remains under hot dispute. Some argue that any benefits from such therapies are down to the placebo effect, which is where a treatment improves symptoms simply because the person using it believes it will, rather than because it has any genuine therapeutic effect.

However, there is a growing body of evidence that the mind and body are inextricably interlinked, and that mental stresses and strains can affect physical health, while physical health problems can affect mental health. For example, stress can trigger conditions like IBS, migraine and eczema; people suffering from illnesses like heart disease, arthritis or cancer often suffer from depression and low self-esteem. Also, it could be argued that, unlike relatively new drug treatments, complementary therapies have stood the test of time, having been used to treat ailments and promote wellbeing for thousands of years.

This chapter gives you an overview of complementary therapies that will give you the boost you need to help you feel more positive about yourself and suggests techniques and treatments you can try including the Alexander Technique, aromatherapy, Bach Flower Remedies, emotional freedom techniques (EFT), homeopathy and massage.

45. Perfect your posture with the Alexander Technique

A person with low self-esteem is likely to hunch their shoulders and look down at the ground, whereas a person with high self-esteem is more likely to hold their head high. You can instantly give your self-image a boost simply by improving your posture, and the Alexander Technique can help you do this.

The Technique was developed in the 1890s by Australian actor Frederick Matthias Alexander, after he realised he was tensing his muscles and adopting an unnatural posture in response to physical and emotional stress before a show, and that this was having a negative effect on his performance.

Poor posture can lead to neck, shoulder and back pain, as well as headaches, all of which could affect your self-esteem. The Alexander Technique aims to improve posture and enable the body to function with the minimum amount of strain on the joints and muscles, helping to relieve muscular tension and pain. It does this by focusing on restoring the correct positioning of the head, neck and back – 'the core' of the body.

The Technique teaches you to become aware of your posture, movement and thinking, as well as any tension in your body, and how to overcome unhelpful habits. Because the Technique encourages you to focus on how your body is feeling *now*, it also helps you to live mindfully in the present, which benefits you psychologically.

To ensure that you adopt the correct posture, it's best to learn the Alexander Technique from a qualified teacher. They will assess your posture and movement, and show you how to rectify any bad habits so that you can move more freely and naturally. Once you have become proficient you will be able to practise at home. Your ultimate goal will be to naturally hold your body in the correct stance all the time.

However, in the meantime, here are three exercises you can try to help you regain your natural poise, ease muscular tension and give your self-esteem a healthy boost.

Stand up straight
1. Stand with your hands by your sides and your feet hip-width apart; distribute your weight evenly between both feet.

2. Ensure your knees feel relaxed, not locked backwards.

3. Position your head correctly to loosen the neck muscles and lengthen the spine: imagine the crown (upper back) of your

head being pulled upwards, while your chin drops and your forehead rolls slightly forward.

4. Your body weight should fall mainly on your heels and your torso should face straight ahead.

Walk tall

1. Adopt the standing position outlined above.

2. As you walk, focus on your weight shifting from one foot to the other, making each movement as effortless as you can. Again, your heels should bear most of your weight.

3. Ensure your upper body is upright, not leaning forwards.

4. A foot should lead each step, not your torso or chin.

Release muscular tension

1. Identify which muscles are tight.

2. One by one, mentally tell each muscle to 'let go', imagining the tension just melting away.

46. Use aroma power

Aromatherapy is based on the idea that inhaling the scents released from essential oils affects the hypothalamus, the part of the brain that controls the glands and hormones, thus altering mood.

When used in massage, baths and compresses, the oils are also absorbed through the skin into the bloodstream and transported to the organs and glands, which are believed to benefit from their therapeutic effects.

There's a growing body of evidence to back up these claims; a study in 2005 at the Medical University of Vienna, Austria, reported that participants who were exposed to floral scents used three times as many positive words in written tests than those who weren't. In 2009, Japanese researchers found that linalool, a component of lavender, lemon, orange and basil essential oils, lowers levels of the stress hormone cortisol in the bloodstream.

Probably the best oils to help raise self-esteem are those that boost mood, create calm and encourage sound sleep. Below is a selection of oils with one or more of these properties:

Bergamot
Bergamot has a wonderfully uplifting citrus aroma, and also has relaxing and soothing effects.
Caution: use in one per cent dilution, as in higher strengths it can make your skin more sensitive to sunlight and more likely to burn.

Lavender
It's widely known that lavender's sedative qualities aid relaxation and sleep, both of which are essential for healthy self-esteem. It also has anti-depressant and pain-relieving properties, making it a great all-rounder to give your physical and mental wellbeing a boost.

Melissa
Also known as lemon balm, melissa is calming and is said to 'chase away black thoughts'.

Sandalwood
Sandalwood's distinctive sweet woody perfume has made it a popular ingredient in perfumes and toiletries. It is both mood boosting and calming and helps to relieve stress.

Massage oil

A two per cent dilution is normally used for massage oils: this equates to two drops of essential oil for each teaspoon of carrier oil. Stronger oils may need to be diluted more, this is mentioned where necessary below. Sweet almond and grapeseed oils are popular carrier oils, but you could also use good quality olive, sunflower or sesame oil from your kitchen. See Action 47 for more about massage.

Never apply aromatherapy oils to broken skin. Buy the best quality essential oils you can afford; like most things, you get what you pay for; cheaper oils may not be as pure as more expensive ones and are more likely to be mixed with solvents or synthetic oils. If you have sensitive skin it is a good idea to do a patch test before using an essential oil you haven't used before; apply a few drops of diluted oil to the inside of a wrist or elbow, or behind an earlobe. If there is no reaction within 24 hours it should be safe to go ahead and use the oil.

Soak in a soothing, aromatic bath

Fill the bath with comfortably warm water. When you are ready to get in, add six drops of your chosen essential oil (unless otherwise stated). Swirl the water around with your hand to disperse the oil, which will form a thin film on the water. The warmth of the water both helps absorption through the skin and releases aromatic vapours, which are then inhaled.

Steam inhalation

This method is good for when you feel you need to clear your head or when you have a headache. Add three to four drops of your chosen oil to a bowl of very hot – but not boiling – water. Lean over the bowl and carefully drape a large towel around your head and the bowl, then inhale the vapours for a minute or two.

Caution: Supervise children while using this method, to ensure they don't scald themselves.

Make a compress
A hot compress is a great way of easing tense muscles, especially in the neck, shoulders and back, and also works well for headaches. Soak a facecloth or handkerchief in a basin of hot water to which you have added four or five drops of your chosen oil. Wring out the excess moisture and apply to the painful area.

47. Boost your mood with massage

Massage is probably the oldest technique used for promoting and maintaining general wellbeing; there's evidence that ancient civilisations such as the Egyptians, Romans and Greeks used it for its pain-relieving and relaxing properties.

> **Tip**
>
> For a quick and easy way to enjoy your favourite essential oil, add about 20 drops to a bottle of your favourite shower crème or bath foam. Shake well before each use.

Massage stimulates the release of serotonin and endorphins, which not only help to relax the mind and relieve pain but also boost mood and self-esteem. Massage also relieves the stress-related muscular tension that can build up in the neck and shoulders, loosens and stretches the muscles, and boosts the circulation. Ask your partner or a friend to give you a massage and then offer to reciprocate;

warm your chosen massage oil between your palms before applying to the neck, shoulders and back, using one or more of these basic massage techniques:

Stroking/effleurage – using gentle to firm pressure, move both hands over the skin in rhythmic fanning or circular movements.

Kneading/petrissage – using the thumbs and fingers, squeeze then release the flesh.

Friction – using your thumbs, apply even pressure in small, circular movements.

Hacking – using the sides of your outstretched hands alternately, deliver short, sharp taps all over.

48. Tap into emotional freedom techniques (EFT)

The emotional freedom techniques (EFT), like acupressure and acupuncture, are energy therapies based on meridian theory; this is the idea that life energy, or qi, flows along 22 channels in the body known as meridians. An even passage of qi throughout the body is viewed as essential for good health. Disruption of the flow of qi in a meridian can lead to illness at any point within it. The flow of qi can be affected by various psychological and lifestyle factors, including stress, emotional distress, diet and environment. EFT are often known as 'psychological acupressure' due to the similarities between the two therapies.

According to EFT, many of us hang on to negative emotions, which are then stored in the meridians, where they disrupt the flow of energy and trigger more negative thoughts. The techniques are derived from the Chinese system of chi kung, which involves tapping on particular points to rebalance the energy flow throughout the body.

In EFT you repeat a statement out loud that describes your negative emotions in a way that makes you feel more positive and encourages self-acceptance, while tapping particular points on your meridians. It is claimed that this sends a pulse of energy through the meridians, which releases your negative emotions. A similar technique, called thought field therapy (TFT), has been adapted and used by well-known hypnotherapist Paul McKenna to help people overcome anxiety, stress and food cravings. Celebrity fans of EFT include Madonna and Lily Allen. To use the techniques to boost your self-esteem, try the following steps:

1. Describe a negative belief you have about yourself. For example: 'I think I am worthless'. Next, to help you feel more positive about yourself, and practise self-acceptance, reframe this statement with the words 'Even though… I deeply love and accept myself', so that the statement becomes: 'Even though I believe I am worthless, I deeply love and accept myself.' If your self-esteem is so low that you can't bring yourself to say 'I deeply love and accept myself', try saying 'Even though I find it difficult to say I deeply love and accept myself, I am willing to learn to deeply love and accept myself'.

2. Using the tips of your index and middle fingers, tap five times on the 'side of eye' meridian points, situated on the outer bony part of the eye sockets where the eyebrows end. Stimulating this point is said to promote calm. As you tap, repeat your

statement, so that you focus on the negative beliefs or thoughts you hold about yourself.

3. Using your right index and middle fingers, tap five times on the left 'underarm' meridian point, situated under your armpit, in line with your nipple. Repeat on your right side using your left index and middle fingers. Stimulating these points is said to relieve worry, aid concentration and speed up thought processes. As you tap, repeat your statement to help you focus on the negative thoughts or beliefs you want to let go of.

For more information and an EFT tapping points diagram go to: www.theenergytherapycentre.co.uk/tapping-points.htm.

49. Use flower power

Every single person has a life to live, a work to do, a glorious personality, a wonderful individuality.

Dr Edward Bach

Flower essences have been used for their healing properties for thousands of years. However, it was Dr Edward Bach, a Harley Street doctor, bacteriologist and homeopath, who developed their use in the twentieth century. He was one of the first modern medical practitioners to treat the cause of disease rather than the symptoms.

Bach believed that negative emotions were the root cause of illness and that the mind, body and spirit had to be in total harmony for physical and mental wellbeing. He identified 38 basic negative states of mind and created a plant or flower-based remedy for each. The remedies are designed to encourage wellbeing by combating negative emotions, such as fear, despair and uncertainty, but there's only anecdotal evidence that they work.

The remedies are made by steeping flower heads in spring water in direct sunlight, or by boiling twigs from trees, bushes or plants. Brandy is added to the infusion to act as a preservative and to produce a tincture. The remedies can be taken mixed with water, or you can use them neat dropped onto your tongue or rubbed onto your lips, temples, wrists or behind your ears. They're widely available in pharmacies or health shops such as Holland & Barrett in handy-sized 10 ml and 20 ml phials. Below is a list of Bach remedies that you may find helpful when your self-esteem needs a boost.

- **Bach Rescue Remedy** – this combination of rock rose, impatiens, clematis, star of Bethlehem and cherry plum is designed to stabilise the emotions and to restore inner calm, control and focus at times of acute stress, such as before an exam or job interview. It is also available as a spray, a cream (which also includes crab apple), as pastilles and as chewing gum.

- **Crab apple** – helps to overcome self-loathing and low self-esteem.

- **Larch** – helps to build confidence in your abilities to help you overcome fear of failure and reach your full potential.

- **Mimulus** – helps to dissolve fears and worries and promote a positive state of mind.

- **Pine** – helps to improve self-worth, especially in people who feel inferior to others and suffer from feelings of guilt and self-blame.

For further information on how to select a suitable flower remedy, and an online questionnaire that enables you to select a personalised blend, visit: www.bachfloweressences.co.uk.

50. Get help from homeopathy

Homeopathy means 'same suffering' and is based on the idea that 'like cures like' – substances that can cause symptoms in a well person can treat the same symptoms in a person who is ill. For example, coffee contains caffeine, which in excess can overstimulate the mind and cause nervousness and insomnia, so the remedy coffea is often prescribed for these very symptoms.

According to homeopaths, symptoms such as inflammation and fever are signs that the body is trying to heal itself. They believe that homeopathic remedies encourage this self-healing process and work rather like a vaccination – because their effects mimic those of the illness they are designed to treat – this approach is completely the opposite to conventional medicines, which aim to suppress symptoms.

Homeopathic remedies are made from plant, animal, mineral, bark and metal sources. These substances are mixed with a solution of alcohol and water and left to stand for several days or even weeks. The mixture is then strained through a filter, or squeezed through a press to produce a liquid known as the 'mother tincture'. One drop of the mother tincture is then diluted with pure alcohol and distilled water and succussed, i.e. shaken vigorously, or banged on a hard surface, many times over to increase its potency. Once the mixture is at the right dilution and potency a few drops are added to base tablets.

Paradoxically, homeopaths claim that the more diluted a remedy is, the higher its potency and the fewer its potential side effects. They say this is down to the 'memory of water', i.e. the theory that even though the molecules from a substance are highly diluted, they leave behind an electromagnetic 'footprint' – like a recording on an audiotape – which has the same effect on the body as the original substance.

There are two main types of remedies – whole person or patient based and symptom based. It's probably best to consult a qualified homeopath who will prescribe a remedy aimed at you as an individual, based on your personality, as well as your symptoms. However, if you prefer, you can buy homeopathic remedies at many high street pharmacies and health shops.

These ideas are controversial and many GPs remain sceptical; a report in 2009 by the Science and Technology Committee of the UK Parliament concluded that while some homeopathic remedies appeared to make patients feel better, it was likely this was due to the placebo effect. However, the British Homeopathic Society argues that there is a growing body of evidence to show that homeopathy has a beneficial effect on 77 different health problems including depression, anxiety and insomnia.

Below is a list of three homeopathic remedies, along with the psychological and physical symptoms often associated with low self-esteem, for which they're commonly recommended. To self-prescribe, simply choose the remedy with indications that most closely match your personality traits and symptoms.

Follow the dosage instructions on the product. The remedies are usually in tablet form and are taken by allowing them to dissolve under the tongue. Avoid eating for half an hour before or after taking a homeopathic remedy, to aid absorption.

Anacardium orientale
Made from: Marking nuts, which grow in India, Malaysia and Indonesia.
Emotional symptoms: Feelings of unworthiness and inferiority; feeling the need to prove yourself.
Physical symptoms: Digestive problems; eczema.

Aurum metallicum
Made from: Gold
Emotional symptoms: Perfectionism; workaholicism; feelings of worthlessness and anxiety; oversensitivity to criticism.
Physical symptoms: Headaches, irregular heartbeat.

Lycopodium
Made from: Stag's horn moss (also known as wolf's claw, or club moss).
Emotional symptoms: Fear of failure and of being left alone; general anxiety and apprehension and low self-opinion.
Physical symptoms: Easily tired by physical activity; insomnia.

Practitioners warn that homeopathy isn't a quick fix and the remedies may take a while to work. Homeopathic remedies are generally considered safe and don't have any known side effects, although sometimes a temporary worsening of symptoms known as 'aggravation' may take place. This is seen as a good sign, as it suggests that the remedy is stimulating the healing process. If this happens, stop taking the remedy and wait for your symptoms to improve. If there is steady improvement, don't restart the remedy. If the improvement stops, start taking the remedy again. You may see an improvement within hours, or it could take several weeks or even months, depending on whether your condition is acute or chronic.

To conclude

This book has offered you many suggestions to help you boost your self-esteem, and hopefully you are feeling inspired and ready to make some changes to your lifestyle and the way you think about yourself. The following sections aim to help you do this; there are recipes to help you put the dietary advice into practice, as well as details of useful products, including the supplements mentioned in Chapter 2 that you may want to try. There is also a list of books you may find helpful if you want to learn more about some of the topics covered in this book. You'll also find the contact details, including the web addresses, of organisations that you may want to consult for further information and support.

Recipes

This section features recipes based on the dietary recommendations outlined in this book. All of the dishes are not only nutritious, but also quick and easy to prepare.

Pan-Fried Salmon with Avocado Salsa (serves 2)

In this recipe the salmon provides protein, omega-3 fats and vitamin D to balance the blood sugar and boost mood. The avocado supplies omega-6 and omega-9 fats, vitamins, minerals and fibre.

Ingredients
For the salsa
1 small avocado, peeled, stoned and cubed
8 cherry or baby plum tomatoes, chopped
1 tbsp fresh coriander, finely chopped
Half a small red chilli, finely chopped
Juice of half a lime
2 tbsp olive oil
Sea salt and black pepper

For the salmon
1 tbsp olive oil
2 skinless and boneless salmon fillets
2 wedges of lime

Method
Salsa
Mix the avocado, tomato, coriander and chilli together with the lime juice, 2 tbsp olive oil and sea salt and black pepper to taste.

Salmon
Heat the olive oil in a small frying pan on a high heat and fry the salmon fillets for about 2-3 minutes on each side, or until cooked through. Serve with the avocado salsa and a wedge of lime.

Mediterranean Chicken (serves 2)
In this recipe the chicken supplies protein to boost serotonin levels and balance the blood sugar. The potatoes, courgettes, red onion, peppers and plum tomatoes provide fibre and antioxidant vitamins A, C and E, while the olives provide antioxidants and omega-9 fats.

Ingredients
250 g baby new potatoes, washed and thinly sliced
1 large courgette, sliced diagonally
1 yellow pepper, de-seeded and cut into chunks
1 red pepper, de-seeded and cut into chunks
1 red onion, peeled and cut into wedges
8 firm plum tomatoes, halved
12 black olives, pitted
Sea salt
Coarse ground black pepper
2 skinless, boneless chicken breasts
3 tbsp olive oil
1 tbsp torn basil leaves or rosemary sprigs

Method
Preheat oven to 200°C/gas mark 6/fan oven 180°C. Place the

potatoes, courgette, onion, peppers and tomatoes in a shallow roasting tin and scatter over the olives. Lightly season with salt and coarsely ground black pepper. Make 3–4 cuts in each chicken breast with a sharp knife, then place on top of vegetables. Spoon olive oil over the chicken and vegetables, then sprinkle with torn basil leaves or rosemary sprigs. Cover roasting tin with foil and cook for 20 minutes. Remove foil from tin. Return to oven and cook for a further 10 minutes until the chicken is thoroughly cooked and golden.

Mixed Bean Chilli with Brown Rice (serves 4)

In this recipe the beans and brown rice provide slow-release energy, protein, fibre and B vitamins, for a balanced mood, while the peppers, red onion and tomatoes provide antioxidant vitamins A and C.

Ingredients

300 g brown rice
1 tbsp olive oil
1 red onion, chopped
1 yellow pepper, de-seeded and cut into chunks
1 red pepper, de-seeded and cut into chunks
1 small red chilli, de-seeded and finely chopped
1 garlic clove, peeled and crushed
2 x 410 g cans mixed beans, drained and rinsed
400 g can chopped tomatoes
150 ml vegetable stock
4 tbsp low-fat natural yogurt to garnish

Method

Bring a large pan of water to the boil, add the brown rice and cook as per pack instructions. Heat the olive oil in a large saucepan over a medium heat and fry the onion and peppers for 5 minutes or until the peppers and red onion have softened slightly. Add the chilli and garlic and fry for a further minute. Add the mixed beans, chopped tomatoes and stock. Bring to the boil, then reduce the heat, cover and simmer for 15–20 minutes. Serve the chilli with the brown rice, topped with 1 tbsp natural yogurt.

Wholemeal Tea Loaf

In this recipe the wholemeal flour and the dried fruits provide B vitamins, fibre, minerals and slow-release energy, to maintain a balanced mood. The dried fruits also count towards your five a day.

Ingredients

75 g raisins
75 g sultanas
75 g currants
300 ml tepid black tea
250 g wholemeal self-raising flour
200 g soft light brown sugar
1 free-range egg, beaten
1 tsp ground cinnamon
1 tsp freshly grated nutmeg
Olive oil for greasing

Method

Place the dried fruit in a large bowl. Pour the tea over the top, cover with a clean tea towel and leave to soak overnight. The next day, preheat the oven to 175°C. Mix the wholemeal flour, sugar, beaten egg, cinnamon and nutmeg into the soaked fruit. Grease a 22 cm x 10 cm loaf tin. Spoon the mixture into the tin. Place in the oven and bake for around one hour and fifteen minutes, or until a skewer inserted into the loaf comes out clean. Serve sliced and spread with vegetable or olive margarine.

Jargon Buster

Below are explanations of terms used in this book that you may be unfamiliar with.

Antioxidants – substances thought to neutralise free radicals.

Cortisol – a hormone released by the adrenal glands during the stress response.

Dopamine – a neurotransmitter involved in feelings of pleasure.

Endorphins – the body's own painkillers.

Free radicals – substances produced by normal chemical reactions in the body and linked to cell damage.

Gamma-aminobutyric acid (GABA) – a neurotransmitter, or brain chemical, that promotes calm by reducing brain activity.

Glycaemic index – a ranking of foods according to the effect they have on blood-sugar levels.

Homocysteine – an amino acid found naturally in the body. High levels are thought to increase the chance of heart disease, stroke, Alzheimer's and osteoporosis.

Melatonin – the 'body clock' hormone that regulates sleep and waking.

Neurotransmitter – a brain chemical with a role in the transmission of messages from one nerve cell to another. Some neurotransmitters increase brain activity and others reduce it.

Norepinephrine – a hormone released during the stress response.

Placebo – an inactive substance given to study participants to compare its effects against those of a real treatment.

Placebo effect – a situation where a person taking a placebo feels better because they believe they have received a real treatment, and expect to feel better.

Precursor – a substance used by the body to produce another substance.

Serotonin – a neurotransmitter involved in mood, relaxation, appetite and sleep.

Tryptophan – an amino acid the body uses to make serotonin and melatonin.

Useful Products

Below is a list of products and suppliers that may help to improve your self-esteem. The author does not endorse or recommend any particular product and this list is by no means exhaustive.

Bach Calm Official Flower Remedy Shop
Online supplier of Bach Flower Remedies.
Website: www.bachfloweressences.co.uk

G Baldwin & Co
Herbalist founded in London in 1844. Offers a wide range of herbal supplements, tinctures and tea bags.
Website: www.baldwins.co.uk

Happy Days 5-HTP
Supplement containing 5-HTP, vitamin C, biotin, niacin, vitamin B6, folic acid and zinc.
Website: www.healthspan.co.uk

Holland & Barrett Complete B Vitamin B Complex Caplets
Caplets that supply seven types of B vitamins.
Website: www.hollandandbarrett.com

Kira Good Mood St John's Wort Extract 450 mg

A traditional herbal supplement containing standardised 450 mg of St John's wort extract.

Website: www.thehealthcounter.com

Nature's Best Pure Grade St John's Wort High Strength One-a-Day

Tablets containing 340 mg of concentrated St John's wort extract.

Website: www.naturesbest.co.uk

Nelson's Homeopathic Pharmacy

Homeopathic pharmacy founded in 1860. Sells homeopathic remedies and Bach Flower Remedies online.

Website: www.nelsonspharmacy.com

Prewett's Instant Chicory 100 g

A caffeine-free alternative to coffee made from roasted chicory root.

Website: www.prewetts.co.uk

Serotone – 5-HTP

Supplement containing 5-HTP (50 mg/100 mg) along with zinc and B vitamins.

Website: www.highernature.co.uk

Seven Seas Pulse Omega-3 Pure Fish Oil

Capsules containing 260 mg of omega-3 essential fatty acids and vitamin E.

Website: www.seven-seas.com

Seven Seas Pure Cod Liver Oil

10 ml (2 tsp) provides 400 IU of vitamin D, 828 mg of EPA and 736 mg DHA (omega-3 fatty acids).

Website: www.seven-seas.com

Solgar Formula Vitamin B-Complex '100' Tablets
High-potency tablets containing vitamin B complex.
Website: www.solgar.co.uk

Solgar 5-Hydroxytryptophan (5-HTP)
Supplement containing 100 mg of 5-HTP, along with magnesium, valerian root extract and vitamin B6.
Website: www.solgar.co.uk

Symingtons Classic Dandelion Coffee 100 g
Caffeine-free coffee substitute made from dandelion roots.
Website: www.healthstore.uk.com

Tisserand Aromatherapy
This company offers a wide range of good quality essential oils designed to improve health and happiness.
Website: www.tisserand.com

Vertese Omega Oils 3, 6 and 9
Omega-3, 6 and 9 oils supplement derived from plant sources, making it suitable for vegetarians and vegans.
Website: www.vertese.com

Helpful Reading

Branch, Rhena & Willson, Rob, *Boosting Self-Esteem For Dummies* (John Wiley & Sons, 2009) – a fun-to-read book on using CBT to boost your self-esteem, written by two cognitive behavioural therapists.

Davis, Patricia, *Aromatherapy: An A–Z* (Vermillion, 2005) – a comprehensive guide to essential oils and how to use them to relieve stress and improve your wellbeing.

Harrold, Fiona, *Reinvent Yourself – 7 steps to a fresh new you* (Piatkus, 2004) – a great little book to help you get to know yourself better, decide what you want out of life and to go for it!

Jeffers, Susan, *Feel the Fear and do it Anyway* (Vermilion, 2007) – a life-changing book on how to overcome your fears and turn indecision into action by doing the things you fear.

Tolle, Eckhart, *The Power of Now* (Hodder & Stoughton, 1999) – a thought-provoking book on how to deal with the pressures of twenty-first-century living by staying focused on the present, rather than worrying about the past or the future.

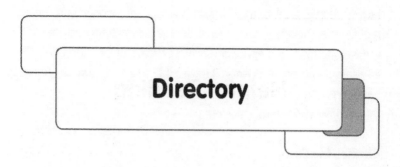

Directory

Below is a list of contacts offering useful information and support with topics and issues covered in this book.

ABC of Yoga
A website offering tips, advice and poses for those who wish to practise yoga at home. Also provides meditation techniques.
Website: www.abc-of-yoga.com

Bigwardrobe.com
Website where you can swap, buy and sell clothes, shoes and accessories.
Website: www.bigwardrobe.com

The Body Control Pilates Association
A website where you can learn about Pilates, find a Pilates teacher and buy equipment.
Website: www.bodycontrol.co.uk

The British Homeopathic Society
Charitable association that aims to promote homeopathy by providing information and supporting research and training in homeopathy.
Website: www.britishhomeopathic.org

Citizens Advice Bureau

Helps people resolve their legal, financial, emotional and other problems by providing free, independent and confidential advice. Visit the website for online advice and contact details for your local CAB.

Registered office: Myddelton House, 115–123 Pentonville Road, London N1 9LZ

Website: www.citizensadvice.org.uk

Clothes for Cash

A website that allows you to recycle your clothes, shoes and accessories, as well as make some cash and help people in the Third World.

Website: www.clothesforcash.com

Freecycle

An online recycling organisation that aims to reduce waste, save resources and ease the burden on landfill sites by encouraging people to give and get unwanted items for free.

Website: www.freecycle.org

Freegle

A recycling organisation that aims to keep anything reusable out of landfill sites by encouraging people to give away and receive unwanted items for free.

Website: www.ilovefreegle.org

Health Supplements Information Service

Service that aims to provide accurate and balanced information on vitamins, minerals and food supplements.

Address: 52a Cromwell Road, London SW7 5BE

Email: info@hsis.org

Website: www.hsis.org

International Stress Management UK

ISMAUK is a registered charity and the leading professional body representing a multi-disciplinary professional health and wellbeing membership in the UK and the ROI. It promotes sound knowledge and best practice in the prevention and reduction of human stress. It also sets professional standards for the benefit of individuals and organisations using the services of its members.
Telephone: 0845 680 7083
Email: stress@isma.org.uk
Website: www.isma.org.uk

Medicines and Healthcare products Regulatory Agency (MHRA)

A government agency responsible for ensuring that medicines and medical devices work, and are acceptably safe.
Address: 151 Buckingham Palace Road, London SW1W 9SZ
Telephone: 020 3080 6000
Email: info@mhra.gsi.gov.uk
Website: www.mhra.gov.uk

Mental Health Foundation

UK charity that provides helpful information and carries out research on the causes, prevention and treatment of mental health problems, including depression, low self-esteem and stress. The foundation also campaigns for, and works to improve, services for anyone affected by mental health problems. It takes an integrated approach to mental health that incorporates both social and biological factors. Online resources include downloadable podcasts on stress and relaxation. The charity's Be Mindful campaign offers information on reducing your stress levels by using mindfulness, an online mindfulness course and details of mindfulness courses across the UK.
Address: Mental Health Foundation, London Office, 9th Floor, Sea Containers House, 20 Upper Ground, London SE1 9QB
Telephone: 020 7803 1100
Website: www.mentalhealth.org.uk

Mind

A national charity for people with emotional and mental health problems – including low self-esteem; offers information and advice online, as well as through a network of local Mind associations that provide counselling, befriending and drop-in sessions, etc.

Address: 15-19 Broadway, Stratford, London E15 4BQ
Telephone: 020 8519 2122
Helpline: 0845 766 0163 (local rate, Monday to Friday, 9.15 a.m. – 5.15 p.m.)
Email: contact@mind.org.uk
Website: www.mind.org.uk

The Money Advice Service

Helpline: 0300 500 5000, (Monday to Friday, 8 a.m.–6 p.m. except bank holidays; typetalk 18001 0300 500 5000)
Address: The Money Advice Service, 25 The North Colonnade, Canary Wharf, London E14 5HS
Email: enquiries@moneyadviceservice.org.uk
Website: www.moneyadviceservice.org.uk

Money Saving Expert

A website dedicated to saving people money on anything and everything, by finding the best deals and beating the system. Created and run by leading financial journalist Martin Lewis.
Website: www.moneysavingexpert.com

NHS Direct

NHS website offering an online initial assessment, where you can check your symptoms and get health advice, including advice on mental health issues such as depression and low self-esteem. The website links to NHS Choices, which has a 'healthy living' section with advice on mental wellbeing, including mindfulness. You can also find out about psychological therapy services, such as counselling and CBT, near you. Useful online tools include workplace stress, mental health and lift-your-mood video walls, where people share their experiences via video clips. There are also blogs and forums on specific health topics (NHS Choices Talk), including mental health issues, such as low self-esteem and depression.

Helpline: 0300 123 2000 (8 a.m.–10 p.m., seven days a week)
Website: www.nhsdirect.nhs.uk

Really Worried

A website where you can seek or share help and advice on just about any worrying topic.
Website: www.reallyworried.com

Relaxation for Living Institute

A charity which offers information on stress and its effects on the body, as well as relaxation techniques. Also provides a database of Relaxation for Living Institute teachers and relaxation classes across the UK.
Address: Relaxation for Living Institute, 1 Great Chapel Street, London W1F 8FA
Telephone: 020 7439 4277
Website: www.rfli.co.uk

The Society of Teachers of the Alexander Technique (STAT)

Website that provides information about the Alexander Technique, including the latest research, a database of Alexander Technique teachers, and details of courses and workshops across the UK.
Address: 1st Floor, Linton House, 39–51 Highgate Road, London NW5 1RS
Telephone: 0845 230 7828
Website: www.stat.org.uk

The Stress Management Society
The Stress Management Society is a non-profit-making organisation dedicated to helping people tackle stress. The website offers a wealth of information about stress and how to deal with it.
Telephone: 0844 357 8629
Email: info@stress.org.uk
Website: www.stress.org.uk

50 THINGS YOU CAN DO TODAY TO BOOST YOUR CONFIDENCE

Wendy Green

ISBN: 978 1 84953 411 6

Paperback   £6.99

In this easy-to-follow book, Wendy Green explains how life events and experiences, as well as lifestyle and psychological factors, can affect your confidence, and offers practical advice and a holistic approach to help you develop strong self-belief, including simple dietary and lifestyle changes, and DIY complementary therapies. Find out 50 things you can do today to boost your confidence including:

- Be body-confident by eating well and exercising regularly
- Control stress to feel more self-assured
- Challenge confidence-sapping thoughts and beliefs
- Exude confidence with the right body language, speech and image
- Overcome your fears by stepping out of your comfort zone
- Learn to feel confident in real-life situations
- Find helpful organisations and products

Wendy Green is a health project co-ordinator and health promoter. She is the author of several health books including *50 Things You Can Do Today to Manage Stress* and *50 Things You Can Do Today to Manage Anxiety*.

Have you enjoyed this book?
If so, why not write a review on your favourite website?

If you're interested in finding out more about our books, find
us on Facebook at **Summersdale Publishers** and follow us on
Twitter at **@Summersdale**.

Thanks very much for buying this Summersdale book.
www.summersdale.com